CW00520021

NO CONSOLATION

RADICAL POLITICS IN TERRIFYING TIMES

David Ridley

Peter Lang

Oxford • Bern • Berlin • Bruxelles • New York • Wien

Bibliographic information published by Die Deutsche Nationalbibliothek.
Die Deutsche Nationalbibliothek lists this publication in the Deutsche Nationalbibliografie;
detailed bibliographic data is available on the Internet at http://dnb.d-nb.de.

A catalogue record for this book is available from the British Library.

A CIP catalogue record for this book has been applied for at the Library of Congress.

Cover image: David Ridley.
Cover design by Brian Melville for Peter Lang.

ISBN   978-1-80079-595-2-(print)
ISBN   978-1-80079-596-9-(ePDF)
ISBN   978-1-80079-597-6-(ePUB)

© Peter Lang Group AG 2022

Published by Peter Lang Ltd, International Academic Publishers,
Oxford, United Kingdom
oxford@peterlang.com, www.peterlang.com

David Ridley has asserted his right under the Copyright, Designs and Patents Act, 1988, to be
identified as Author of this Work.

This publication has been peer reviewed.

'In case you were wondering, no, there's nothing defective about our shared sense of reality right now. The world is burning, refugees are drowning, the seas and atmospheres are turning toxic and billions of workers around the world are now struggling to cover the basic costs of living. Yet all the while the future's disappearing, shareholder dividends and payouts to the wealthiest have never been higher.

But that's no reason to think it's all about to collapse, far from it. One family's crisis is an investment banker's windfall bonanza. For as long as people look simply for consolations – comforting beliefs about the future that offer false certainty in exchange for inaction and disengagement – business continues as it always has. And pretending that a clever policy fix or a magical collapse through internal contradictions will settle the matter insults the intelligence, hopes and desires of each of us.

This fiery, startling yet engaging polemic is an injunction to think and act together. Eschewing glib or easy answers, Ridley builds on his experiences as a political activist to think about how we got here, while visioning ahead to a near future of reaction, struggle and opportunity. Read this and be prepared to think it all again, upside down, inside-out– together. Rip it up and start again.'
– Dan Taylor, Lecturer in Social and Political Thought, Open University and author of the Orwell Prize shortlisted book *Island Story: Journeys Through Unfamiliar Britain.*

'Books on what's wrong with our reactionary political class and the unjust unequal system that they protect and promote, abound. This book is special; it is about the fundamentals of resistance. It starts from the creative, intelligent agency of ordinary people. This book is an essential resource for the resistance now growing.'
– Hilary Wainwright, Red Pepper co-founder and author of *Arguments for A New Left: Answering the Free Market Right.*

'"We have all been stumbling through our lives since 2008," David Ridley says in his preface to this densely argued but very readable book. Its four chapters present "interventions" to unravel the confusions inflicted upon young people most directly facing climate change, economic crisis and war. Only their collective intelligence can transform the "strange world" imposed by "radicalised neoliberalism" where you "buy your own truth" in commodified schools, colleges and universities. United with students and communities, Ridley concludes that education workers can recover their collective power to nurture a new future–a blast of hope against the consolations of despair.'
      – Patrick Ainley, former Professor of Training and Education at the
      University of Greenwich and author of *Betraying a Generation: How
      Education is Failing Young People.*

'No Consolation is an incisive text that offers a critical and historical understanding of present-day political crises, and how we might change them. Engaged in dialogues about youth politics, the coronavirus pandemic, climate change, and universities, Ridley sharply weaves together these topics to ask pressing questions such as "what do we do when climate crisis is seen as another investment opportunity?"

Importantly, and paired with its predecessor *The Method of Democracy*, this book articulates a range of transformative practices about what we might 'do' collectively to make things better. As Ridley says, it's scary out there, but we can change it, together, "building a new world, from the bottom up".'
      – Kirsty Morrin, Lecturer in Sociology at the University of Liverpool
      and co-editor of the book, *Inside the English Education Lab: Critical
      Ethnographic Perspectives on the Academies Experiment.*

For Stephen

Contents

Preface: Blah Blah Blah

At the time of writing, over 6 million people have died across the world because of the coronavirus pandemic.[1] More than a hundred million jobs were lost in 2020 compared to the previous year,[2] while schoolchildren around the world had missed just under two trillion hours of in-person learning by September 2021.[3]

Inequalities have deepened even further. Young people, women and minorities already struggling to make ends meet in neoliberal societies have been the most severely impacted by the pandemic. Often working in sectors like retail and hospitality on precarious contracts with little protection, they have either lost their jobs or been forced to continue working at greater risk of contracting COVID-19.[4]

Nevertheless, the wheels of the capitalist world economy have kept on turning. Online retailers and entertainment giants like Amazon and Netflix have made a killing, becoming even more powerful than before. While people were losing their jobs or worrying about whether they would still be employed after furlough schemes were withdrawn, financial markets boomed. During the pandemic, markets like the S&P 500 Index – which tracks 500 of the largest companies listed on US stock exchanges – and the Dow Jones Industrial Average reached record highs.

One of the positive stories we heard during lockdown was the rediscovery of nature by the busy commuters of the modern world. We went on walks, worked in our gardens, listened to birds tweeting and worried about our impact on the environment. As a result, governments have been talking about 'building back better' – but what has this actually translated into?

'Blah, blah, blah. Green economy. Blah blah blah. Net zero by 2050. Blah, blah, blah.' This was youth climate activist Greta Thunberg in a speech in September 2021, a year and a half after the pandemic hit the West. 'This is all we hear from our so-called leaders. Words that sound great but so far have not led to action. Our hopes and ambitions drown in their empty promises,' she continued.[5]

For the largest, consumer-facing corporations – the Nestlés, P&Gs and Unilevers – climate change is now a marketing opportunity, a way to grab market share in a post-pandemic, pre-apocalyptic world. Building back better, even the Green New Deal – once a Trojan Horse for a socialist 'just transition' – are now slogans touted by the organic intellectuals of monopoly finance capital.

One of the conclusions of this book, which was written 'on the hoof', so to speak, is that we are witnessing a *neoliberal restoration*, not the long-awaited and longed-for death of neoliberalism and its replacement by something better. True, a war is being waged between progressive and reactionary sections of the ruling class, with the green capitalists and neo-Keynesians on one side and the oil barons and right-wing populists on the other. But whichever side wins, we, the people, will lose.

I say that the book was written 'on the hoof'. What does that mean? I was in the middle of another book, on higher education, thinking that the pandemic would pass and the world would soon return to normal. But as the crisis wore on, and we Brits went into our third lockdown during winter 2020, I knew I had to understand what had happened, how the world had changed. So, I started reading. Not the early analyses of the left, but the conversation going on within the ruling class, in the reports of consultants like KPMG and McKinsey, and in the articles of *The Economist* and *Financial Times*.

It is this 'inductive' method that explains the structure of the book. It was impossible to describe the situation as it was emerging in logical, argumentative terms. So instead, I had to think in terms of 'interventions' – each chapter is, in a way, a separate essay on the pandemic from a particular point of view or problem. These 'themes' are idiosyncratic, they are based on what I saw as important. But I think we need a bit more personality in our critiques, don't you? This is also why a near future narrative frames the book, to soften some of the edges of the theory.

Nevertheless, a grand narrative did begin to emerge. Of a generational crisis, in which two cohorts – the Millenials and the so-called Pandemials – were lumped with the effects of not one, but two global crises. People who, like me, came of age in the 90s and 'noughties' have had their lives, particularly their careers, turned upside down by the 2008 Financial Crisis. For me, it was particularly bad timing, as I'd just graduated as a mature student in Philosophy. It took me two years to get a job, and another six to find one secure enough to get a mortgage. And I was lucky.

We have all been stumbling through life since the 2008 crisis, which seemed to shake the very foundations of the capitalist world economy. But the system crawled on, pretending that everything was fine. The crisis was blamed on the centre-left, and the costs were socialised through austerity. The world kept warming and money circulating, through debt and speculation, rather than via wage growth and investment. But it wasn't fine. Brexit, Trump, Corbyn, Black Lives Matter – these were all attempts to make this very clear, in a way that couldn't be ignored.

And then the pandemic hit, out of nowhere. Well, out of the same unsustainable system of reproduction that had produced the last crisis.[6] But anyway, the virus raged through an already shattered world, ravaging health systems that had been cut to shreds and punishing people who had already been left behind by a privatised and marketised public sector.

This 'creative destruction' may be good for business, but as Chapter 1 explains, it's bad for the kids. The next generation of workers and graduates will also have their careers 'scarred', which is to say they will earn less over their lives and find it harder to get on those all-important ladders of social mobility. But for this generation, and for those at the very bottom of the ladder, the rungs are already broken.

None of this will be lost on this new 'lost generation'. Young people are already pissed off, at the failure of adults to do anything about climate change, at the racism that still festers openly on the streets and within our institutions, at the false promise of higher education and 'human capital' to give them a leg up, when in fact, all they do is put you in your place within the 'pear shaped' tower block of modern life.

Another 'meta' theme that runs through the book is the 'consolation' of intellectuals – not just left-wing ones, but also the 'traditional' intellectuals of neoliberalism. I take this term, *consolation*, from the work of early twentieth century philosopher John Dewey, a term that he used to describe a social and psychological tendency in which people erect theoretical fortresses of certainty to compensate for the chaos and absurdity of reality.[7]

We see this again and again on the left. Frustrated by the failure of history and real people to follow the logic of revolution laid out in an endless series of books, left-wing intellectuals write even more books, looking for even cleverer ways to explain the world in the hope that this will inspire revolutionary action.

We are all guilty of this, to a certain extent. Isn't our obsession with Netflix boxsets, online gaming, modern board games, internet shopping, dogs, cats, food, beer, beards, wellness, mindfulness, self-help, self-care – aren't these all forms of consolation? Aren't we all avoiding the truth that the world is shit and if we could really be bothered, we could actually change it?

And here's me writing a book on it! Isn't that a form of meta-consolation? Maybe. But as Ludwig Wittgenstein said, a book can also be a series of pointers to help people 'see the world aright'.[8] Philosophy is 'nonsensical' and serves a function. Like a ladder. This time to truth not success. After use, the ladder should be 'thrown away' (or perhaps recycled).

For conservatives threatened by change, and by a new generation threatening change, consolation can take much more dangerous forms. The contents of today's ideology are naturalised and eternalised, nostalgia compensates for chaos and order is sought in authority. In Jordan Peterson's academic work, for example, contemporary values like entrepreneurialism, individualism and knowledge are found in the pre-reflective, mythical origins of collective consciousness. The job of the conservative intellectual, reimaged as mythical hero, is to dive into tradition, rediscover the organic, experiential basis of our (patriarchal/Christian, White/Anglo Saxon) values and thereby renew the basis of popular, legitimate and stable rule.[9]

Bubbling beneath the surface of society is a nastier, darker and more violent version of this new ideology. In the anonymous subgroups and chat rooms of online communities, an army of vulnerable, alienated people of all ages are being groomed by neo-fascists. Here consolation becomes resentment, and sometimes, egged on by the irony of the 'edgelords', a 'truther' takes action in the real world.

Anders Breivik's killing spree in Norway in 2011, including sixty-nine members of a Workers' Youth League (AUF) summer camp, was inspired by a variety of internet-based conspiracy theories that blame Muslims, feminists and 'cultural Marxists' for a European 'cultural suicide', which he collated into his own influential manifesto, *2083: A European Declaration of Independence*.

Brenton Tarrant's 2019 mass shootings at two mosques in Christchurch, New Zealand were influenced by supremacist 'Great Replacement' conspiracy theories, propagated in YouTube videos and by alt-right influencers like Tucker Carlson, which argue that white people are being exterminated by a cosmopolitan, Jewish elite via immigration and forced assimilation, and are being made to feel guilty about being white by liberal 'woke' politics and multiculturalism.

Most recently, Jake Davison's murder of five in Plymouth, UK, in 2020, which included his mother and a 3-year-old girl, has been linked to the misogynistic online involuntary celibates or 'Incel' subculture. Whether or not the murders were directly motivated by this ideology, Davison was a prolific YouTube content producer, and made reference to ideas like 'black pilling' – a trope within this culture that signifies an Incel's acceptance of their inability to attract members of the opposite sex – which in turn symbolises a deeper nihilism, as well as the more general antifeminism and rape culture of the online 'manosphere'.

But even in the darkest corners of the world there can be a glimmer of hope. While there can be no excusing the acts described above, or the content of the ideologies that provide their motivation and the conduits for far-right manipulation and grooming, these online communities all share a common desire to find the truth in a fundamentally dishonest world. This truth-seeking is driven not by evil or, in my opinion, even hate, but by *alienation*.

These people, many of them young, have no hope. They have not only been left behind by meritocracy but see through its false promises. The moment of conspiracy thinking is also the beginning of critical thought. It is our job, therefore, as progressives, intellectuals, educators, parents,

friends, colleagues and neighbours, to help people find the real truth, and
to do this in a way that promotes openness to the world and its difference,
genuine solidarity, mutual respect and friendship – exactly the opposite
of how the far right operates when it preys on the vulnerable.

We need to rediscover our *collective intelligence*, by fighting battles
and winning and then building movements out of these specific causes.
When we come together to fight and win, we don't just make the world
a better place, and thereby shatter the hold of pessimism, cynicism and
what Mark Fisher called 'capitalist realism'.[10] We also create institutions
that pool our individual experiences, knowledge and capacities that form
the foundations of radical democracy.

This is our truth. It is what is denied by both neoliberal and reactionary ideologies. It is the real alternative to the market, which doesn't
intelligently match supply and demand through a mysterious, computer-
like price mechanism, but in fact redirects wealth and power to the already wealthy and already powerful, while creating chaos for everyone
else. Unfortunately, however, this alternative has also been forgotten by
the left, by the centrists seeking a softer neoliberalism and by the radicals
who have given up hope in the masses.

I've tried to point to where collective intelligence provides an alternative or way forward out of the specific issues that frame each chapter. But
if you want to understand this concept more fully, I recommend you read
my last book, *The Method of Democracy: John Dewey's Theory of Collective
Intelligence*. In this book, I reconstruct a theory of collective intelligence
out of Dewey's work, setting this theory against both the slippery free
market ideology of neoliberalism and the pessimism of academic critical
theory, and propose an alternative practice of intelligent democracy as a
way out of the mess we find ourselves in.

Before we move on to the first chapter, I'd like to take this opportunity
to thank a few people who made this new book possible. Firstly, Stephen
Cowden, who reassured me that the project was worthwhile, just when
I had convinced myself it was going nowhere and might become another
unfinished book. Secondly, Eamon Gamee, with whom I discussed many
of the ideas in the book, and who made me realise that 'truthing' was something not to be dismissed, but to be considered critically, and potentially

even positively. And by extension, the whole Beyond Education editorial collective, who during the pandemic, embodied the idea of collective intelligence for me and also provided a model of dialogic publishing that we are trying to take forward with the new Interventions series.

I'd like to thank Patrick Ainley and the Post-16 Educator editorial board for making me understand that education doesn't create jobs or fuel growth in capitalist societies, and that it is the lack of investment in our collective future that has got us into this mess. In particular, I'd like to thank Post-16 Educator editor Colin Waugh for always believing in my research and providing a space to work out many of the ideas in this book.

I'd like to thank Tony Mason for believing in both the book and the new series, and to Peter Lang for taking a chance with it.

And of course, I can't forget my partner, Helen, who has listened to me ramble on about Dewey, Marx and education for many years, and whose criticisms of the ideas in this book during our many lockdown walks were always well placed.

In the middle of the third decade of the twenty-first century, the neoliberal restoration had begun to collapse. Despite shifting significantly to the right to meet the challenge of a growing international neo-fascist movement, conservatives in the global North started to lose their grip on power. Increasingly authoritarian and repressive measures, such as herding asylum seekers into offshore concentration camps, in all but name, sacking critical academics, expelling student activists from universities and banning progressive literature from schools, could not prevent neoliberal hegemony from collapsing – not just in the hopes and dreams of left-wing intellectuals, but this time, in reality.

However, this was not something to celebrate. In the UK, a new force emerged to take its place: the Arthurian Knights. Partly a continuation of the right-wing populist movements of the post-2008 years, the Arthurians rejected the fundamental premises of neoliberalism. The market was a euphemism for a system controlled by an international financial elite, populated by lizards or Jews, depending on what faction you spoke to at any given time. People weren't consumers, they were citizens of a nation with a shared purpose, which needed to be discovered through action and the radical reconstruction of social and moral values. The state was not a servant of global capitalism but of the Anglo-Saxon race, whose material and spiritual needs trumped every other consideration.

Led by the 'charismatic' King Arthur (who looked like a cross between a football hooligan and a late nineteenth century greengrocer – think Tommy Robinson meets Greg Wallace), the Arthurians appealed to a strange collection of supporters. On the one hand, there were the Tory defectors, mostly retired, terrified of crime, climate change, you name it. But also angry at the Conservatives for leaving them to die from COVID-19 and taxing them as part of this 'just transition' or whatever the liberals were calling it. On the other hand, there were the Labour Party defectors; baby boomers whose material base had been destroyed by deindustrialisation and whose children looked upon the apparent successes of first, second and third generation migrants with furious envy. On the fringes were also a new generation of unemployed, under-employed and self-employed 'Pandemials' who couldn't afford a mortgage, spent most of their time on social media and were happy to see someone doing something, especially about those bloody condescending 'wokeflakes'.

'We need to protect our Anglo-Saxon heritage and reinvent the organic tradition that this heritage represents and carry it into the future,' reads the latest edition of the Arthurian propaganda rag, the Magna Carta. 'Britain has fallen foul of a mob of woke leftist bullies that want to destroy our values. They are a cult; they want to hurt sensible traditional working-class people. They want to punish our children for being white. We represent the English heroes that in 2016 stood up to this liberal conspiracy and their immigrant army by voting to take our country back. But this achievement has been corrupted by the other side of this countermovement – the shady bankers and stock-market gamblers represented by the complacent and corrupt Tory party. The Arthurians will follow through what we started, create a new social and political order in the country and make being proud to be English something we can shout about again.'

CHAPTER I

Change Is Coming Whether You Like It or Not

In the 1960s and 1970s, Pierre Bourdieu published a series of books with his colleague Jean-Claude Passeron critically examining the French education system at the time. In their classic analyses they found that, rather than offering a means of social mobility for working class entry into the capitalist middle class, the French republican state education system in fact acted like a sorting mechanism, placing, on the one hand, working class youth where they belonged, in boring, insecure and poorly paid jobs, and on the other, entry into the corridors of power for the upper middle classes, thus ensuring that the ruling class reproduced itself from generation to generation.[11]

More than this though, by promising social mobility through working hard on oneself through education, and with all now able to access education through the state, education becomes the very institutionalisation of capitalist ideology. Taking their place in a long line of post-war critical theorists – Gramsci, Horkheimer, Adorno and Althusser – Bourdieu and Passeron deepen the Marxist theory of ideology by exposing its materiality, that it is not just a distortion of reality expressed in the ideas, images and theories of popular culture, but a shaper of reality itself. More than perhaps any other theorist of ideology, Bourdieu in his life work traces the relationship between economic structures, state and non-state institutions, and the habits and common sense of everyday life, albeit perhaps, like many Marxists, weighting this relationship in favour of structure over agency.

The problem with this kind of critical theory, however, is that it creates an ideological closed circle. Instead of being liberating, these exposés of the capitalist system end up only confirming its power. This is a criticism often made of 'functionalist' Marxism, but Jacques Rancière – a contemporary of Bourdieu often lumped in with other French poststructuralist theorists like Michel Foucault – comes at this from an interesting and

extremely pertinent angle. Rancière's early work is concerned with exposing the 'stultifying' effect of critique and with uncovering instead the
capacity of ordinary people to not only understand their own domination,
but to imagine their own alternatives.[12] Rancière criticised Bourdieu and
Passeron's theory of reproduction on the basis that it creates a conceptual
tautology, which he sets out as follows:

1   The system reproduces itself because it is misunderstood.
2   By reproducing its existence, the system generates an effect of
    misunderstanding.[13]

Applying this to education: working class children don't go to university
because they are sorted by the education system into the kind of people
who go to university, and those who don't. A complex interaction between 'cultural capital' – the knowledge and habits that children bring
from their family and social backgrounds – and the institutional processes and structures of schooling make the exclusion of working-class
children from higher education a self-fulfilling prophecy. Their necessary failure – as well as the exceptions that prove the rule – confirms,
socially and psychologically, that this was not their destiny in the first
place, that everything is working as it should be.

The perfection of this ideological mechanism, the very success of its
sorting of those who should 'think' (rule, teach, create) from those who
should just 'do' (work, learn, consume) is also what ensures the working
class will never understand its manipulation, thus preventing it from
being able to imagine something different, and overthrow this system
in favour of something better, fairer – a system that works for it, rather
than against it. This is essentially the 'truth' that is uncovered by critical
theorists, that it is impossible to break out from ideology from within,
exactly because of its reproductive perfection. But how does the critical
theorist escape ideology? Well, that's the magic of the critical theorist,
and the source of their power. The intellectual *just is* the person who can
see through ideology, and whose job it is to expose, again and again, the
perfection of its reproduction.

Left-Wing Pessimism

What Rancière exposes so brilliantly in his essay 'The Ethics of Sociology', therefore, but also in other important works like *The Ignorant Schoolmaster* and *The Philosopher and his Poor*, is the place of the intellectual within the system of ideological reproduction. Here Rancière echoes Gramsci, who was keen to distinguish between what he called 'traditional' and 'organic' intellectuals.[14] The latter are intellectuals that arise out of an organic social formation – that is, a group or class that is an active element in the struggle for control over the means of reproduction in any given epoch – and work to give this formation ideological coherence and self-consciousness. By contrast, traditional intellectuals, in many cases the organic intellectuals of a by-gone era, try to remain outside the realm of struggle and ideology, so that they appear to be in a position of 'Olympian detachment'.[15] But this is not really the case, Gramsci insists, and in the struggle for socialism, if these intellectuals are not won over to the anti-capitalist cause, they will, wittingly or unwittingly, act to sustain the status quo.

For Rancière, then, the problem with critical theory is not so much its content, but its 'performative' effect.[16] Rancière describes this as follows: 'It is impossible to imagine that this order could ever cease contributing by its very existence to its own perpetuation.'[17] For anyone still reading critical theory today, this might recall the left-wing cliché: 'It is easier to imagine the end of the world than it is to imagine the end of capitalism.'[18] This phrase is meant to capture the way that neoliberal ideology sought to capitalise on the fall of communism in Russia in the 1990s and the transformation of socialism in countries like China and Vietnam into a new, authoritarian state capitalism. Thatcher's phrase 'there is no alternative' – often shortened to TINA – and Francis Fukuyama's 'end of history' thesis serve as exemplifications of this for the intellectual left.[19] But critical theory tracts, with their combination of lengthy, withering critique and small-scale solutions, the latter often tacked onto the end as afterthoughts, only end up reinforcing this sense of hopelessness in the face of overwhelming complexity and embedded power.

Interestingly, however, at the end of *Les héritiers* – Bourdieu and Passeron's first book on education – a crack in this closed circle of ideology appears. They conclude in the Epilogue that instead of perfectly sorting those who think from those who work, French higher education in the 1960s was actually drawing attention to its function within capitalist reproduction. By over-promising social mobility, the 'baby boomers' whose parents wanted more for their children than the drudgery of mass production still found themselves in boring, proletarian jobs as 'factory workers or postmen', despite working hard and graduating from the country's best universities.[20] Furthermore, both working class kids and the children of the bourgeoisie found universities to be strangely factory-like in the way that lecturers attempted to pour knowledge into lecture halls full of eager receptacles, like water into empty jugs, or perhaps more like mincemeat into sausages, to use Marx's metaphor.[21]

As a result, instead of successfully instilling capitalist ideology in young people – that you get what you deserve – education during this era engendered 'disillusionment' within a new 'bamboozled' generation.[22] This disillusionment might, Bourdieu and Passeron suggested, turn into social unrest. The following passage from the Epilogue – published in French in 1964 – is worth quoting in full:

> The structural deskilling of a whole generation, who are bound to get less out of their qualifications than the previous generation would have obtained, engenders a sort of collective disillusionment: a whole generation, finding it has been taken for a ride, is inclined to extend to all institutions the mixture of revolt and resentment it feels toward the educational system. This anti-institutional state of mind (which draws strength from ideological and scientific critiques) can lead in extreme cases to a denunciation of the social order, a practical suspension of doxic adherence to the prizes it offers and the values it professes, and a withholding of the investments which are a necessary condition of its functioning.[23]

Just four years later, this is, of course, exactly what happened. In May 1968, workers joined students on the streets of Paris in a showdown over the very foundations of the French social order which very nearly became another French Revolution.[24]

Within the same text, then, we have, on the one hand, the beginnings of a totalising critique of ideology which no one can escape except intellectuals, and on the other, the possibility that young people might escape this ideology, without their help.

Youth of Today

Although the revolutions of the 1960s failed to overthrow capitalism, the cracks in capitalist ideology identified by Bourdieu and Passeron have only widened in the last five decades. In his own *Les héritiers* for today, *Betraying a Generation*, Patrick Ainley traces a similar disillusionment in British youth coming of age in the wake of the 2008 Financial Crisis. While young people may no longer have to dread a life of drudgery working in the same factories as their parents, they can now instead look forward to years stuck in low-paid, insecure and boring jobs in retail and hospitality. This is despite the increasingly grand promises made for education, especially higher education, for which almost half of 18-year-olds now take on tens of thousands of pounds of debt for. Wiping 6 per cent of GDP from the UK economy and pushing the unemployment rate up to 8.4 per cent, the highest rate since 1995, the 2008 Financial Crisis left a new generation of graduates 'overqualified and underemployed', Ainley argues, and, like their French equivalents half a century earlier, finding that their qualifications 'do not guarantee middle class jobs, merely admission to the pools that are allowed to compete for these jobs'.[25]

The years following the 2008 crisis saw little improvement for young people. According to the Trades Union Congress, four out of five jobs created during the period following June 2010 were 'low-skilled, low-paid and often part-time insecure jobs in sectors such as retailing, waitressing and residential care, with an average hourly rate of £7.95 or lower'.[26] Obscuring real unemployment figures, self-employment within what is now referred to as the UK's 'gig economy' increased from 3.8 million in 2008 to 4.6 million in 2015. Within this figure, part-time self-employment grew by 88 per cent.[27] Meanwhile, young people and parents have seen higher education as a means to ride out the immediate storm created by the crisis and as a way to secure access to the diminishing pool of decent jobs, perhaps even a professional career. But the result has been a race to the bottom. Half of graduates in the UK labour market are unable to find a graduate role. According to the Office for National Statistics, there were 8.2 million degrees in 2013, but only 6.8 million jobs requiring degree.[28]

And of course, more graduates competing for non-graduate jobs pushes more non-graduates out of employment completely. Youth unemployment has persisted at a much higher level since the crisis. In October 2014, it remained at 16 per cent for those in the 16-to-24 age group – nearly three times the adult rate of 6 per cent.[29] Even based on the number of 18- to 24-year-olds not in full time education, youth unemployment was 12 per cent, double the general rate.[30] 'Despite the gospel of salvation through education, changes in work and occupations have increased inequality and reduced the certainty of employment,' Ainley concludes. 'For the majority of the younger generation, this had led to a serious mismatch between employment opportunities and their educational qualifications, expectations and aspirations. Instead of moving up, many young people face the possibility of downward social mobility into low-paid, low-skilled employment, so that the risk of being "underemployed" is at least as great as being unemployed.'[31] Young people coming of age in the wake of the Financial Crisis, then, feel increasingly like they are 'running up a down-escalator', Ainley says, trying to get ahead in a class structure that he describes as being now shaped more like a pear than a pyramid.[32]

For youth in the wake of the coronavirus pandemic, the future is even bleaker. The conditions described by Ainley have largely determined who has suffered the most, particularly due to the economic impact of the lockdowns imposed to stop the spread of the virus (see also next chapter). According to the Resolution Foundation, the social and economic impact of the pandemic has been 'U shaped', which is to say that the youngest and the oldest have been most affected.[33] The reliance of young people in particular on poorly paid and insecure retail and hospitality jobs – exactly those industries most devastated by lockdown – has meant that they have borne the brunt of the immediate negative economic impact, with one in three 18- to 24-year-old employees losing work or being placed on furlough, compared with one in six older adults.[34] While the UK's Job Retention Scheme prevented these economic impacts turning into mass unemployment in the short term, the Foundation predicted that we would be heading for somewhere between 11 per cent and 17 per cent of 18- to 29-year-olds being out of work when the scheme was withdrawn.[35] This is the same level as in 1984, at the height of Thatcher's war on the British working class.[36]

Drilling down into COVID-related youth unemployment by education level, we get a clearer picture of how a degree is not only today a minimum requirement for work per se, but also a way for young people to shield themselves from recession. At the end of last year, compared to a relatively high rate of 13 per cent unemployment among young people holding a degree (8 per cent between October and December 2019), the proportion of young people with no qualifications that were unemployed rose from 24 per cent in 2019 to 33 per cent in 2020.[37] For those with only GCSEs the rate was also comparatively very high, rising from 15 per cent to 19 per cent over the same period.[38] While the ONS warns that these statistics should be used with caution, as they are based on samples, they paint a depressing picture of the deepening educational divide in Britain. While for graduates leaving education during a recession, the likelihood of being in employment three years after having graduated is about 13 per cent of what it would have been had the economy not contracted, for those with mid-to-lower-level qualifications, these figures are 27 per cent and 37 per cent less likely, respectively. In other words, the Resolution Foundation notes, 'not only is the size of the recession's impact on employment larger for the lowest-qualified, but it lasts longer too.'[39]

But it is the long-term effects of this educational divide that we should be worried about. Echoing what was said earlier about the 2008 Financial Crisis, the Foundation warns that graduates will once again 'trade down' to lower-skilled occupations to ride out the crisis, pushing out many non-graduates into unemployment.[40] However, graduates also get stuck in these low-paid, insecure jobs, undermining one of the only remaining mechanisms of social mobility. 'Voluntary job-to-job moves (i.e., following resignation rather than redundancy) plummeted in the Financial Crisis and were slow to recover, particularly at younger ages,' the Resolution Foundation notes. 'Worryingly, between 2018 and 2019 the mobility rate actually fell, by 5 per cent overall and by 8 per cent for 18- to 29-year-olds. This lack of job mobility when young is concerning because such moves … are an important way to progress careers and increase earnings.'[41] Today, many of the lower-paying roles that education leavers have tended to enter during their first years in the labour market are still operating way below pre-crisis levels and are unlikely to reach full capacity in the near future, the organisation continues. 'In other words, the first rung of the employment ladder looks to be broken, and it is unclear when (if ever) it will be mended back to recent conditions.'[42]

This deepening intergenerational crisis will further undermine another key tenet of neoliberal ideology: that British society is a 'property owning democracy'.[43] Almost half of young people aged 18- to 29-years-old still live with their parents.[44] First-time buyers need to save an average of twenty-one years to afford the deposit required for a typical UK home.[45] As a result, one in five households are rented, double that at the turn of the century.[46] The problem here is that, with the insecurity of renting and the dramatic rise in rental prices due to property speculation and social housing shortages, many young people, and especially young families, are being pushed into poverty. In 2018/19, more than a third of private rented households (37 per cent) were in poverty, increasing from 35 per cent a year before.[47] Combined with a fifth of people working in retail and hospitality suffering from in-work poverty, more and more young people are looking forward to a life of misery.[48] No matter how hard you work, if you are a working-class youth, it is extremely likely that you will have to visit a food bank or take out a loan to pay the bills. This is in one of the richest countries in the world.

Generation Left

It is my belief, therefore, that the impulse for social change in the wake of the pandemic will come from young people. This should not be a revelation to left-wing intellectuals; even right-wing economists recognise this possibility, and more importantly, fear it. For example, youth disillusionment is identified by the World Economic Forum as one of the gravest risks facing the capitalist system over the next few years, for exactly the reasons described above.[49] 'Pandemials are at risk of becoming the double lost generation of the 21st century,' the organisation argues.[50] Taking a global view, the WEF points out that even before COVID, children and youth accounted for two-thirds of the global poor, with a third of young people across the world not even completing primary school.[51] With regards to youth employment, the situation elsewhere echoes that of the UK: 'Many young adults work in the sectors hardest hit by the pandemic,' the WEF points out, 'such as the service industry and manufacturing, often on part-time or temporary contracts with limited job protection. Altogether, the number of young people who are not in employment, education or training (NEETs), already at 21 per cent in early 2020, is likely to rise in the coming year.'[52]

All of this will translate into youth disenfranchisement, the WEF worries, 'amplified by disappointment at the slow economic recovery from the 2008 Financial Crisis, frustration at ostensibly corrupt and ineffective elites, and socio-economic fault lines that have exposed deep-rooted injustices.'[53] What is interesting about the WEF's analysis is that it not only recognises the threat posed by youth disenfranchisement, but that this disenfranchisement has already manifested itself as political struggle. The WEF points to the growing number of youth-led movements that have 'erupted' in the past decade, listing the Arab Spring, global climate strikes, and Black Lives Matter as three high-profile examples. We can add to these the 2010-11 student movement in the UK and elsewhere, the global Occupy movement, the pro-democracy movement in Hong Kong, and the Dakota Access Pipeline protests (which we will hear more about in Chapter 3). Because of these movements, we arguably saw the radicalisation of mainstream left and/or left-liberal parties in the UK and US, for example, the Labour Party under Jeremy Corbyn and the campaign to get Bernie Sanders elected as Democratic candidate during the 2020 US presidential elections.

If we look at exit poll data from the latest US election, the last two UK parliamentary elections and the 2016 EU referendum, we see a clear divide between younger and older generations with regards to voting patterns. In the 2020 US elections, 62 per cent of voters aged 18- to 29-years-old voted for Joe Biden, compared to 48 per cent of over 65s.[54] The divide is even starker in the UK. In the 2019 election, 16 per cent of 18- to 24-year-olds voted Labour, compared with 22 per cent of 60- to 69-year-olds and 40 per cent of over 70s.[55] 'In fact, for every ten years older a voter is, their chance of voting Tory increases by around nine points, and the chance of them voting Labour decreases by eight points,' YouGov's Adam McConnell and Chris Curtis point out, analysing the 2019 exit polls. 'The tipping point – the age at which a voter is more likely to have voted Conservative than Labour – is now 39, down from 47 at the last election.' The difference was also evident at the EU referendum, although not as extreme. 71 per cent of 18- to 24-year-olds voted to Remain, compared with 36 per cent of over 65s. 'In the EU referendum and again in 2017, age was a new dividing line in British politics,' McConnell and Curtis conclude.[56]

By education, however, the EU referendum exit polls paint a different picture. '70 per cent of voters whose educational attainment is only GCSE or lower voted to Leave, while 68 per cent of voters with a university degree voted to Remain in the EU,' McConnell and Curtis note. 'Those with A levels and no degree were evenly split.'[57] Education levels also mattered in the 2017 and 2019 general elections. In 2019, Labour did much better than the Tories among those who have a degree or higher, by 43 per cent compared to 29 per cent. This echoed the results of the previous general election, but, interestingly, Labour did slightly better among the lower educated than two years later, with 33 per cent of people educated to GSCE level or below voting Labour in 2017 compared to 25 per cent in 2019.[58] Furthermore, in 2017, 40 per cent of 'medium educated' people voted for Labour compared to only 31 per cent in 2019. However, we must also remember that only about half of young British people actually vote. Polling research from Ipsos MORI shows turnout among 18-to-24-year-olds in the 2017 election was only 54 per cent, falling to 47 per cent two years later.[59]

What the above suggests is that there is a youth legitimacy crisis in rich democracies like the UK and US, one which will be exacerbated by the pandemic and its deepening of insecurity and intergenerational inequality.

The Method of Democracy

The key question for activists is how this crisis can be translated into something positive. What I describe above is a standard Marxist macro-theory of contradiction, which I think sets the scene for post-pandemic social life. However, while macro-level crises loosen the grip of ideology and expand the realms of the possible, there is no guarantee that they will produce progressive consciousness. As with the examples noted in the Preface – Breivik, Tarrant and Davison – the very inequalities that structure capitalism's illusory 'meritocracy', alongside a dearth of vehicles for constructive expression, often mean that the experience of crisis turns inwards, rendering people vulnerable to manipulation by reactionary forces. What we need is an account of how macro-contradictions are experienced by individuals, and how this individual experience can be collectivised and channelled into political causes aimed at changing the very conditions that produce these contradictions in the first place.

In my most recent book, *The Method of Democracy*, I proposed a theory of 'micro-contradiction' that explains this process, based on the work of early twentieth-century philosopher John Dewey. For Dewey, existence is in a state of permanent flux. Organisms from bacteria to human beings are in biological terms attempts to establish order within chaos. This evolutionary dialectic, or 'rhythmic alternation', as Dewey calls it, between relative permanence and ceaseless change is the origin of all creativity and intelligence. Human intelligence is merely the most developed, and infinitely adaptable, expression of this struggle against chaos, and one that transforms the ecological relationship so that we create our own environments, introducing our own chaos into the system in turn. Through cultural evolution, social relations now have a greater impact on our own existence than natural flux, as well as on pretty much all other life on Earth, for better or worse. It is no coincidence, therefore, that forms of social inquiry, from science to critical theory, arise, historic-ally speaking, in step with the growing complexity of social life. As part of cultural evolution, Dewey argues, we create institutions – 'collective habits' – to help us pool our collective intelligence and maintain order within this growing chaos.

The problem, however, is that the tools and institutions of collective intelligence have become distorted by the same forces that create the negative consequences they are designed to deal with. To put it bluntly, institutions have become captured by class interests, and have become tools of class hegemony rather than means for public self-understanding. We will return to this point in Chapter 4, in relation to universities. For now, it is important to note how firstly, intelligent collective action emerges 'naturally' out of the experience of social contradiction, and secondly, how this process requires collective inquiry to change conditions in the future.

Compare the following examples. You get dressed for work. You put on your shoes and a shoelace snaps. This is a minor inconvenience that can be solved by either replacing the shoelace, or, if a replacement isn't immediately available, putting on different shoes. All of this can be done within the flow of habitual action, with no reason to engage in any reflection on the problematic situation that has arisen. Your car then breaks down on the way to work. You are not a mechanic, so you must call a mechanic to come out and fix it so that you can get to work. This is disruptive, annoying and maybe stressful. But solving this problem is still relatively straightforward, requiring in most cases no extended reflection on the conditions that produced this problematic situation. Breakdowns are to be expected; this is why we have breakdown insurance.

Now consider unemployment. You finally get to work and find out you are being made redundant. This is the kind of problematic situation that can create a full-blown existential crisis, fundamentally unmooring you from the flow of everyday life for an unbearable period of time. It is often these kinds of social breakdowns that produce negative behaviours, especially when there is no constructive outlet for the feelings generated. Immediately, the things you take for granted flash before your eyes: your bills, your mortgage perhaps, the financial solvency of your household if your family depends on your income; all of this is coloured by a deep anxiety – unless, of course, you are in shock – an anxiety that is compounded by an empathetic projection onto those who depend on you: how this will impact them? how they will feel about you? how will you feel about yourself? and so on. No longer grounded by the material foundations of habit, you may spiral into a pattern of self-destructive behaviour, escalating into new, negative habits, such as unhealthy eating, excessive drinking, drug abuse, which all produce negative reactions in those you love, intensifying these bad habits, perhaps eventually resulting in obesity, alcoholism, violence, self-harm, and/or depression.

These are all common, understandable reactions to such incredibly stressful experiences. But they are all also expressions of the futility of individual action in the face of social contradiction. While an individual may find help in therapy to stop engaging in self-destructive behaviours and habits or find solace in religion or self-care to recover a sense of hope, these will not address the source of the problem. Only by engaging in intelligent, collective action can the origins of negative consequences be identified through co-inquiry and the means of preventing these negative consequences from arising in future be identified and enacted.

What does this look like? Well, in the case of unemployment, you might turn to a trade union to find out if there is anything you can do to fight the redundancy you are facing. You might find out that there is, in fact, a collective response to the situation, and your colleagues, who are also in the union, are negotiating with management to see if the redundancies can be avoided. Management, however, are being intransigent, and are interested in only preserving profitability in the face of a difficult economic context. So, together you decide to take collective action, a strike perhaps.

For some this is not necessarily an example of collective intelligence. Unions can be bureaucratic and led by charismatic personalities. They are not always democratic, and strikes can sometimes be counterproductive. This is all certainly true, but in my experience, the decision to act collectively to improve material conditions is always a difficult one, and usually comes at great personal risk, both economically and emotionally. But the reward is potentially huge, not just economically, but for way that the experience of taking collective action transforms you. It breaks the hold of what Mark Fisher called 'capitalist realism' – the idea that there is no alternative – and brings you out of the alienation and cynicism that can be so mentally exhausting, without even realising.

Perhaps most importantly, intelligent collective action also transforms our relationships with others. When we take the risk of changing social life to make things better for others as well as ourselves, we create and experience *solidarity* – a form of interpersonal bond that is generated through collective action and is qualitatively different from the kinds of alienated relationships we experience on a day-to-day basis.

In summary then, the grim economic and social situation facing young people today has the potential to turn a whole generation against the status quo. Two global crises – the 2008 Financial Crisis and the coronavirus pandemic – have made the future for many uncertain, anxious and almost certainly worse than in the past. Combined with hollow promises from leaders invested in maintaining the existing order, this situation is shattering the ideology that has dominated politics and social life for over thirty years. Any number of specific issues – unemployment, education, climate change, war – could provide the spark that brings people together to fight for a better world. If we can find ways of linking these struggles through practices and institutions of collective intelligence, we could build a movement capable of winning something fundamentally different.

However, the neoliberal ruling order will not give up without a fight. As we will see in the next two chapters, the ruling class is constantly adapting and shifting its ideology to rationalise further exploitation and inaction on the key issues we face, and is constantly trying to obscure the truth in order to prevent us from creating and nurturing our collective intelligence. In fact, the very foundations of neoliberalism depend on a denial of collective intelligence, as we will see.

'We used to make things in Coventry,' Joe said to his son as they walked back from the protest they had just disrupted. The protest was about climate change, again. Self-righteous middle-class lefties telling everyone else that they should stop buying things, going on holiday, eating meat, and whatever else. Joe didn't want to hurt anyone – the anti-protest had got a bit out of hand – but someone needed to stop all this political correctness, it was destroying society. And they are just so condescending, telling everyone else how to live. What if you can't afford an electric car, to buy organic food – and why shouldn't we take advantage of cheap flights to go abroad? 'People used to travel from across the world to work in our car factories,' Joe continued, 'because the wages were so high. That was ok, the car industry was booming, there were plenty of jobs to go around and the wages were good. But now, there aren't any jobs. Look at you, son, you went to college to do one of these new apprenticeships and now you can't get any work, cuz everyone else had the same idea and there weren't really the jobs in the first place – it was just another one of these hairbrained government schemes, designed by people who have never had to do an honest day's work in their lives. Now I'm delivering Amazon parcels and you're working in Sainsburys!'

'It's ok dad, I don't mind,' Ben said. But he did mind. He hated working in Sainsburys, it was so boring and he was sick of being told what to do by his manager, Justin, who was actually shit at his job and used to stack shelves with him, but because he had a degree, had been promoted over him. Ben didn't really like going on the protests, but didn't want to disappoint his dad, who was a bit of a King Arthur fanatic. His dad was retired, and when he wasn't working as a self-employed delivery driver to top up his meagre state pension, he was on YouTube, watching Magna Carta and Jordan Peterson videos, soaking up every last drop of anti-woke vitriol. Thinking about the protest, Ben thought it was strange that the police just stood by and did nothing. He didn't want to get arrested, but some of the anti-protesters were pretty nasty and really hurt people. Ben disagreed with the lefties, and spent a lot of time on the Internet arguing with them on Facebook and Twitter, but he thought, if you resort to violence, then you've lost the argument. He just wanted to know the truth. He knew that the government was lying to *him about just about everything, and he thought that education just filled people with silly ideas. But he also didn't trust all these alt-news networks and chat rooms either. 'Everyone's got an agenda,' he thought to himself. 'How are you supposed to know what's real?'*

CHAPTER 2

We Live in a Strange World Where You Can Buy Your Own Truth . . .

During spring 2020, most people across the world were in either full or partial lockdown, as governments tried to stem the tide of coronavirus infection. These lockdowns and related border closures seized up the interconnected global market, wiping roughly 15 per cent real gross domestic product – GDP adjusted for inflation – from the world economy.[60] To put that into context, the COVID-19 recession was the deepest since the end of the Second World War, and more than twice as deep as the recession associated with the 2008 Financial Crisis.

While the interconnected nature of the world economy means that no country has been immune to the effects of this global recession, it is worth noting that some countries and regions, unsurprisingly the poorest, have fared worse than others. For example, by September 2020, Peru and Ecuador had the highest number of excess deaths per million people, with Mexico not far behind.[61] It's not surprising, then, that the Latin American economy was predicted to suffer the worst economic impact, with per capita GDP in the region to shrink by a devastating 8.1 per cent by the end of that year.[62]

But what is surprising is how badly the coronavirus hit some of the richest economies. The UK, for example, was in September 2020 the fifth worst hit in terms of the highest number of recorded excess deaths, at roughly a thousand per million.[63] After losing a quarter of its non-adjusted GDP between February and April 2020, despite a brief bounce-back over summer, the UK is thought to have lost about 10 per cent GDP over the space of the first pandemic year, more than double the world average.[64]

Why did the UK fare so badly? It is now widely accepted that Prime Minister Boris Johnson, ignoring the advice of scientists (beyond those he appointed), imposed lockdown measures too late.[65] Despite the first confirmed coronavirus cases appearing at the end of January, the UK waited until the middle of March to introduce lockdown measures – one of the latest countries to do so in Europe. Not only did this mean far more deaths than necessary, but it also had the opposite effect to what was intended: minimising the long-term impact on the economy.

Compare the UK with China, for example. The Chinese government imposed strict containment measures almost immediately, including the extension of the national Lunar New Year holiday, the lockdown of Hubei province, large-scale mobility restrictions at the national level, social distancing, and a fourteen-day quarantine period for returning migrant workers. Thanks to these containment measures, China's economy contracted by only 6.8 per cent (year-on-year) in Q1 2020.[66]

Thanks to its swift and decisive interventions, China was predicted to be one of the only countries in the world to achieve the much-longed-for V-shaped recovery and is thought to be the only G20 economy to have grown during 2020. Of course, there are questions about the trustworthiness of China's own data reporting. However, Western hysteria regarding the boost to China's economic power emerging out of the crisis indicates that its recovery is real.

But we can look elsewhere for examples. Australia combined strict lockdowns and proactive testing and tracing to contain the virus, and by November 2020 – the end of winter in the Southern hemisphere – had zero cases. The story in neighbouring New Zealand was very similar. From the first known case imported into New Zealand to the last case of community transmission detected in May, elimination took sixty-five days. Border controls, lockdowns and physical distancing and case-based controls using testing, contact tracing and quarantine together helped the country achieve low case numbers and deaths compared with high-income countries in Europe and North America.

Nudging the Sheep

Key to Australia's success has been science-based, transparent decision-making on the part of government, and a responsible citizenry that willingly and immediately took up the country's containment measures. In other words, the government trusted not just its public intellectuals – that is, those scientists whose research is partly or wholly funded by taxpayers – but also the wider public. Polls showed that trust in government soared to an 'extraordinarily' high level in Australia during the pandemic. Trust in the UK government, on the other hand, sunk to its lowest level in decades.[67]

In contrast to Australia, the UK government, then, has shown not only a (typical) contempt for its public intellectuals, but also for its citizens. Rationalising the UK government's delay in imposing lockdown and social distancing measures, England's chief medical officer, Chris Whitty, said: 'It is not just a matter of what you do but when you do it. Anything we do, we have got to be able to sustain. Once we have started these things, we have to continue them through the peak, and there is a risk that, if we go too early, people will understandably get fatigued, and it will be difficult to sustain this over time.'[68]

Whitty's argument is based on the idea of 'behavioural fatigue', a concept derived from behavioural science. As doctoral researcher at the London School of Economics, Stuart Mills explains: 'As best understood, behavioural fatigue is the idea that eventually people get bored of doing one thing and start engaging in other, sometimes undesirable, behaviours. For example, if people are placed in quarantine, they may initially be very compliant. But after some time, this compliance will wither away.'[69]

However, as 600 UK behavioural scientists pointed out in an 'Open Letter to the U.K. Government Questioning Its Coronavirus Response': 'There is no sound evidence base to suggest that behavioural fatigue would undermine early interventions based on social distancing, and especially not in a case like the one we currently face.'[70] The letter asked the government to make its decision-making transparent and publish its evidence, so that this approach could be scientifically evaluated against the alternative policy of introducing social distancing.[71] While the government eventually relented, and introduced social distancing and lockdowns, it never published this information, so no evidence-based comparison could be made.

In general, what this incident shows is the Conservative Party's recent turn towards a new and insipid form of neoliberal governance: 'libertarian paternalism'. Coined by Richard Thaler and Cass Sunstein in their best-selling 2008 book on behavioural economics, *Nudge: Improving Decisions about Health, Wealth and Happiness*, libertarian paternalism is described by the authors as an approach to policy making that 'preserves freedom of choice but that authorizes both private and public institutions to steer people in directions that will promote their welfare'.[72] David Cameron was so impressed by this book, he set up the so-called Nudge Unit in 2010, a quasi-public think tank now owned partly by the Cabinet Office, Nesta and by employees, which is busy applying nudging techniques to UK social policy as well as marketing its ideas across the world.

A good example of this kind of technocratic governance is asking people to 'opt out' rather than 'opt in' to pensions schemes. Over 90 per cent of eligible private sector workers are now members of workplace pension schemes, thanks to this particular nudge.[73] During the coronavirus pandemic, this approach has been applied to encourage people to wash their hands, suggesting, for example, that we sing happy birthday to measure the time it takes to do this thoroughly, and also to use alternatives to handshaking like elbow bumping. But, as we have seen, it has also been used to justify not taking swift and decisive action in response to the pandemic – a form of 'hard' paternalism, rather than the soft paternalism of nudging – a decision that may have cost thousands of lives.[74]

Science as Ideology

At the core of nudging theory is a conservative assumption about people's intelligence and willpower. While couched in arguments challenging the 'homo economicus' model of human intelligence – that is, that we are all rational actors, and always choose the most beneficial subjective outcomes – the theory posits that we actually have a number of 'built in' biases that lead us to make irrational decisions, often against our best interests. 'Drawing on some well-established findings in social science, we show that in many cases, individuals make pretty bad decisions – decisions they would not have made if they had paid full attention and possessed complete information, unlimited cognitive abilities, and complete self-control,' Thaler and Sunstein write.[75]

As Will Davies points out in his excellent book, *The Limits of Neoliberalism*, the turn to nudging theory can be understood as an attempt to rescue neoliberal ideology, and the hegemonic structures that rest upon it, from the contradictions exposed by the 2008 Financial Crisis. Specifically, it seeks to save the ideal of a rational economic system based upon radical, individual freedom from the 'spectacle of large numbers of individuals exercising their choice in wildly self-destructive and destabilising ways'.[76] Common to all varieties of neoliberalism is an 'assumption that the methodological presuppositions of neoliberalism ought to have been true but are empirically compromised by various anomalies that show up in laboratory experiments, surveys, brains scans or critical situations,' Davies explains.[77]

But what is neoliberalism? The first thing to understand about neoliberalism is that it does indeed exist, contrary to critics who say this is merely a meaningless swear-word of the left intelligentsia.[78] It is definitely overused, we can admit that. But it points to a particular ideological configuration that has dominated politics and economics for the last forty years and more, and has in the last couple of decades exerted a strong and destructive influence over social life and the public sphere. Neoliberalism is an ideology, but as argued in the last chapter, we must recognise that ideologies exert a material force, and are driven – and exposed – by the contradictions of everyday life.

We often hear that 'no one actually calls themselves a neoliberal' – this may be true now, but once upon a time, a group of 'radical' economists used this term to describe their project of reinventing free market ideology for the twentieth century.[79] Originating in a series of *privatseminars* organised by Austrian economist Ludwig von Mises in the 1920s, the neoliberal counter-movement was formed to discredit the intellectual foundations of socialism, which was at the time in ascendance everywhere, from 'Red Vienna',[80] to the then recently established communist state in Russia.

At the core of this neoliberal theory was a critique of economic planning. In its most sophisticated form, in the work of F. A Hayek, this critique takes the form of a more fundamental critique of human knowledge. For Hayek, the 'economic problem of society' is not just the classical liberal problem of allocating resources to meet people's needs – a problem that socialists assumed could be solved through systematic, centralised economic planning – but rather of how to do this when no individual could possibly know what those needs are (including members of the communist party). 'To put it briefly,' Hayek summarised in his hugely influential 1945 essay, 'The Use of Knowledge in Society,' 'it is a problem of the utilisation of knowledge not given to anyone in its totality.'[81]

Tacit Knowing

In his critique of central planning, Hayek uses the concept of 'local knowledge' – knowledge of 'particular circumstances of time and place' – that echoes an idea developed in the work of one-time fellow neoliberal Michael Polanyi. For Polanyi, 'tacit knowing' is a 'fundamental power of the mind, which creates explicit knowledge, lends meaning to it and controls its use.'[82] In Polanyi's view, explicit knowledge, such as science, is dependent on a more fundamental *practice* of knowing and experiencing that guides knowledge creation and application, so much so that 'knowledge' would actually be meaningless without our pre-reflective mode of being in the world.[83]

What Polanyi is describing is a complex 'background understanding' that is both practical and social, with codified knowledge – that is, any knowledge that can be explained, written down, turned into a theory about the world – itself the result of a practice of knowing, rather than just a discovery of something already out there or a reflection of reality.[84] In an important sense, for Polanyi and for other theorists, tacit knowledge can never be codified. This is why Polanyi's work is seen as a radical critique of science, prefiguring later, influential work by philosophers of science like Thomas Kuhn.[85]

While also radical in its critique of central planning, Hayek's theory of local knowledge is very different. It makes no commitments to a social background understanding, emphasising only the individual, dispersed aspects of economic behaviour, which can only be, in his view, coordinated by a supra-individual (but not human) price mechanism. Hayek evokes the figure of the entrepreneur, who uses their savvy grasp of particular opportunities to get ahead of the pack, achieving temporary competitive advantage. He is not really thinking of the skilled worker, who draws upon the collective intelligence of millennia of craft-based production aimed at meeting material and social needs.

It is this *alienated* understanding of how the capitalist system actually works that prevents Hayek from seeing collective intelligence as the real alternative to central planning. Hayek commented that if the price mechanism 'were the result of deliberate human design, and if the people guided by the price changes understood that their decisions have significance far beyond their immediate aim, this mechanism would have been acclaimed as one of the greatest triumphs of the human mind'.[86] But capitalism, and the price mechanism, *are* the result of deliberate human design. All human action is driven partly by habit – both individual and collective – and individual creativity. This is the dialectic of individual and collective intelligence, which operates over vast periods of time.

As Hilary Wainwright points out, 'if knowledge is a social product then it can easily be transformed through people taking action – co-operating, sharing, combining knowledge – to overcome the limits on the knowledge that they individually possess'.[87] This is the truth that Hayek, and neoliberalism more generally, cannot admit, because it leaves open the possibility of planning, at a deeper, philosophical level. We should all admit to the shortcomings of really existing communism, and not pretend that by abolishing private property and democratising production we will have solved the problem of coordinating supply and demand. But this is not the same thing as saying market chaos and inequality are inevitable, or worse, 'natural'.

Collective intelligence is the alternative. Not as a magical system of alienated labour and disembodied commodities floating around the world like information in a computer. But as real people in communities establishing what their needs are and organising themselves to meet these needs through some form of intelligent, decentralised, social planning. There are countless examples of this happening all around the world on various scales right now, as there are many examples of how capitalism actually relies on more planning than neoliberal ideologues would like to admit.[88]

State as Friend, Not Enemy

While Hayek and Mises were tackling economic planning, their Mont Pèlerin Society comrade Willhelm Röpke set about reinventing the liberal theory of the state.[89] Classical liberals believed that the market operated best when left alone. The only things that governments were useful for were protecting individual and corporate private property rights and negative freedoms. All barriers to free international trade should be removed and regulation kept to an absolute minimum.

After the Second World War, however, it was widely accepted that radically free markets didn't work, and by breaking down, had produced the chaos that had allowed fascists to take control in Europe. While Cambridge economist John Maynard Keynes was laying the foundations for a new settlement between labour and capital in the UK, Röpke and other 'ordoliberals' were reimagining the state as a tool for governing 'for the market, not because of it.'[90]

As argued in Michel Foucault's path-breaking 1970s lectures at the Collège de France, ordoliberals realised that the state could actually be far more useful in *promoting* free markets, rather than just protecting them. In contrast to classical liberalism, competition was for neoliberals like Röpke an 'essential economic logic' that would 'only appear and produce its effects under certain conditions which have to be carefully and artificially constructed.'[91]

We have this strand of neoliberalism to thank for 'marketisation' – the policy of introducing markets into places where competition doesn't 'naturally' appear, for example, in education, healthcare, energy and infrastructure. We will see more of this in Chapter 4. We can also see how ordoliberalism and Hayek's epistemological neoliberalism combine to give us nudging theory, which essentially grants governments permission to manipulate us into behaving like good capitalist consumers.

Returning to our story, however, it's with Milton Friedman that neoliberalism's ideological potential is fully realised. In the 1960s, an important shift occurred within the Mont Pèlerin Society, the organisational centre of international neoliberalism. Under the influence of the Volker Fund, the society became increasingly dominated by American economists, and Hayek began to lose interest. Hayek felt that it was no longer the multidisciplinary, internationalist community of inquiry he created alongside Röpke, and the swelling membership undermined the society's function as a clandestine organisation.[92]

Friedman, who had been a part of the Mont Pèlerin Society since its first meeting in 1947, saw an opportunity and staged a successful coup. This resulted in many of the society's European members resigning in protest, and its power centre shifting to the 'Chicago School' of economics. Under Friedman's leadership, the organisation became much more ideologically oriented, and open to political use.

Friedman himself had moved from an initial constructive engagement with socialism and a cautious acceptance of some government regulation – for example, in his 1951 pamphlet 'Neoliberalism and Its Prospects' – to an aggressive and uncompromising advocacy of free markets in *Capitalism and Freedom*. According to Rob Van Horn and Philip Mirowski, he was not ashamed of being 'an intellectual for hire' because for Friedman, 'all intellectual discourse was essentially just a sequence of disguised market transactions.'[93]

What we get with Friedman is a two-pronged approach to reinventing neoliberalism. On the one hand, he attempts to turn economics into an 'objective science' that could make predictions about the world that could be tested in experience.[94] On the other, he renders this new science unfalsifiable, by insisting that the assumptions of economic theory can be false, 'as long as the theory predicts well'.[95]

Here Friedman is cleverly using Karl Popper's 'criterion of falsifiability', which was designed to distinguish science from pseudo-science, to create a pseudo-science out of neoclassical economics.[96] Popper did indeed argue that the existence of factual evidence supporting a theory is not, in itself, reliable proof of a theory. However, while is 'easy to obtain confirmations, or verifications', the 'genuine test' for any theory is a serious attempt to falsify or refute it.[97] A good scientific theory, for Popper, is one that rules things out and makes 'risky predictions' – predictions that can be proved correct or false by reality.

What Friedman proposes, on the other hand, is a model of science where reality itself is undermined on the basis that it fails to conform to the theory. In the case of nudging, for example, the fact that human beings do not always act as rational utility maximisers – that is, selfish consumers – does not undermine the theory, but shows rather that human beings are faulty and need to be adjusted more effectively to the economic order. When this 'as if' methodology is generalised into a full-blown theory of society, all social life is open to manipulation by neoliberal governments and policy makers, whose aim is to move reality closer and closer to ideology.

Beware the Alternatives

Why is all this important? Because it establishes *continuity* between the past and present, and should be a tonic to any leftists that would see neoliberalism's collapse as inevitable with any crisis of reproduction.[98] Neoliberalism will not collapse under the weight of its own contradictions. If anything, contradictions are its lifeblood. Crises are for neoliberal intellectuals opportunities for renewal and retrenchment.

We can see this today, in the way that a certain faction of neoliberals are attempting to profit from the climate emergency, by reinventing capitalism as a progressive, green alternative. As explained in the next chapter, we need to look beyond the ideology of green capitalism to see what kind of alternative is actually being proposed. Does green capitalism challenge the power of financial markets over real production and social need? No. Does it move away from colonial forms of exploitation? No. Does it encourage the development of collective intelligence, nurture radical democracy or shift power from capital to the international working class? No.

Meanwhile, a more sinister version of neoliberalism has appeared in recent years, which seeks to profit from the multiple crises we face in a different way. Some critics see 'right-wing populism' as a challenge to neoliberalism, in particular the latter's technocratic emphasis on elite rule and the depoliticisation of economic and social life. However, as I argue in *The Method of Democracy*, right-wing populism should be seen as a radicalisation of neoliberalism. If we look at the 'fake news' tactics of demagogues like Vladimir Putin or Donald Trump, for example, we can see an extreme version of Friedman's 'post-factual' philosophy, rather than a return to truth telling and reality.

Do right-wing populists challenge the key tenets of neoliberalism? No. When in power, Donald Trump slashed corporation tax in the US, from 35 per cent to 20 per cent. On energy and climate change, he forced a review of Barak Obama's Clean Power Plan, withdrew the US from the international Paris Agreement and restarted works on the Keystone XL and Dakota Access shale oil pipelines (see next chapter). His trade tariffs, which he touted as interventions on behalf of the American working class, were really about instigating a new Cold War with China, and, by increasing the cost of living, did more harm to working class Americans than good. And let's not forget the 'the wall'.[99]

In summary then, neoliberalism is an ideology that adapts and is strengthened by social and economic crises, such as the coronavirus pandemic. Critics and political activists who would like to see it collapse under the weight of global capitalism's contradictions are engaging in a form of consolation. The only way to defeat neoliberalism is to engage in collective action and develop our collective intelligence. This is neoliberalism's weakness, and one that it makes every effort to hide.

But neoliberalism is also a form consolation. One that is open to any defence of the capitalist system. Neoliberals would likely – and have done in many places – even abandon democracy, if it came down to a choice between capitalism and collective intelligence. With the world facing proliferating and increasingly severe crises, particularly related to climate change and its social and economic impacts, this tendency bodes ill for humankind. It is to this challenge, and the ways that people are fighting for real alternatives to neoliberalism, that we now turn.

Most people didn't take the Arthurians very seriously. Despite their new political vehicle – Britain Reborn – coming third in the last general election (2024), helped by the removal of Scotland from the equation (after the Scottish National Party finally delivered a successful independence referendum in 2023, subsequently re-joining the European Union) they were mostly the butt of establishment jokes, sneered on by even the most reactionary sections of the mainstream media. This didn't matter much, however, because they had their own channels on social media, as well as the increasingly powerful and sympathetic Truth TV. (Initially this Murdoch venture was a damp squib. But as the 'culture wars' reached a fever pitch in the lead up to the election, with the 'assassination' of right-wing 'intellectual' Carl Benjamin, aka Sargon of Akkad, by left-wing activists during a university lecture, its audience grew exponentially).

On the other hand, the public was also pretty hostile to the increasingly intransigent climate movement, which had become more and more militant over the last few years. Populated by former Corbynistas and the hardcore of the labour movement's far left, Extinction Rebellion splinter group No Alternative's last action involved shutting down Shell's recently built oil rig off the shore of Scotland. Unlike the Arthurian 'disruption' of climate protests, the police were swift and brutal in their response, arresting the activists involved under new powers granted by the 2021 Police, Crime, Sentencing and Courts Act. While these activists now languish in prison on ridiculously punitive sentences – to 'let young people know that it's time to grow up', according to UK Prime Minister, Priti Patel – Arthurians pose for Instagram pictures in their silly uniforms alongside the Cambo miners, who have welcomed the organisation's permanent militia presence at the site.

For climate activists like Tash, who did not see the direct action of No Alternative as particularly useful, the key question was how to win the public over to a socialist Green New Deal. There was just no way that capitalism could save the world, she thought. All that 'woke capital' cared about was gaining market share in the new green economy. Even if Bill Gates' collection of mini nuclear power plants, waste-powered planes and giant carbon hoovers could keep global warming to $2°C$ (the world gave up on $1.5°C$ after the absolute shit show that was COP27, when Boris Johnson stormed out of the conference hall flipping Greta Thunberg the bird, ranting about how it *was all China's fault), billions of people and animals will die, and the world is going to be fucked for the next generation – 'my generation', she thought, angrily. 'The sooner Elon Musk pisses off to Mars and takes the rest of the willy waving Silicon Valley elite with him the better.'*

'People are just so overwhelmed by the scale of the problem that it's difficult to see how an intergenerational coalition can be built out of the international climate movement,' Tash told delegates at the 2026 World Transformed festival. 'Last year, new petrol and diesel cars were banned, five years ahead of plans, and taxes placed on existing "dirty" vehicles. In the same year, new rules came in for new properties to be built to International Passivhaus Standards, with existing homes given only a year to increase their energy efficiency rating to C or above. In true Tory fashion, little was done to help people manage this transition, and this has pushed people into the open arms of King Arthur. It's true, if it hadn't been for the menacing presence of a radically politicised youth, the Tories would have kicked the climate can down the road for as long as environmentally possible. But if we are going to win this fight, we've got to engage people in our communities on the issues that matter to them – food, housing, work – and build networks of real, material struggle.'

CHAPTER 3

... But It's the Only World We've Got

One morning in January 2014, Murray Paas walked out onto his estate in Queensland to find thousands of flying foxes lying dead on the ground. In a video shared with *The Guardian* newspaper, Paas described what he called the 'massive carnage' from the previous day's 43°C heatwave that swept its way across the central and eastern interior of Australia, as he walked past piles of bat corpses, with many more hanging dead from the trees. Based on the size of his property, he guessed that thousands of bats living in his estate had died.[100] Thanks to a large-scale data-gathering effort, environmental scientists subsequently estimated that at least 45,500 flying foxes had lost their lives in a single day in Queensland, leaving over a thousand orphaned pups to care for.[101]

However, as the researchers pointed out, this was not an isolated event. Between 1994 and 2008, more than 30,000 flying foxes had died in 19 such heatwaves across Australia. Then over two days in November 2018, another heatwave wiped out almost one-third of the nation's spectacled flying foxes – a rare bat species with light-coloured fur around its eyes found only in a small rainforest region of northern Queensland. The heatwave also wiped out another 10,000 black flying foxes, the main victim of the earlier heatwaves, also particularly vulnerable to high temperatures. Lead researcher Justin Welbergen described Australia's flying foxes as the 'the canary in the coal mine for climate change'.[102]

Thanks to global warming, Australia has in recent years also suffered some of the most severe bushfires the country has ever seen. An estimated 100,000 sq. km of land has burned since 2019, killing over a billion animals and at least twenty-eight people.[103] Elsewhere, at the height of the pandemic, dozens of wildfires swept across the west coast of the US, killing more than thirty people, and forcing tens of thousands from their homes.

Another widely shared video showed Charles Bilton and his son Justin trying to make their way back from a camping trip, trapped in their car in the middle of a wildfire in a Montana forest. 'I have never seen anything like it,' Justin said. 'It was just like looking at a war zone – like a nuclear bomb had gone off.'[104]

Meanwhile, the world's ice is melting at a phenomenal rate. According to recently published NASA satellite data, Antarctica and Greenland have together lost roughly 5,000 gigatons of ice over the last sixteen years, contributing to a global sea level rise of about 23 cm since 1880.[105] This doesn't sound like much, but this relatively small rise – alongside other climate-related effects, such as soil erosion and crop failure – has already pushed roughly 700,000 people in Bangladesh out of their coastal communities over the last decade.[106] And then there are the catastrophic weather events, like 2009's tropical cyclone Alia, which killed more than 200 Bangladeshis and displaced millions more.

There are many more examples of how climate change is already happening, disrupting the lives of millions of people, and wiping out whole species of animals. And this is all just with a rise in global temperatures of 1°C. If temperatures rise by 2°C, as they are predicted to very soon, hundreds of millions more people will face starvation due to agriculture loss and food insecurity, will be forced to migrate by rising oceans and will face conflict over scarce resources like food and water. A 2°C rise would also wipe a sixth of global GDP per capita from the global economy.

Beyond 2°C things get increasingly apocalyptic. The more temperatures rise, the more the world risks passing a series of tipping points, setting off changes that will fundamentally shift how the planet behaves. The global ocean circulation system, which helps distribute heat around the world, could break down. The rainforests could turn to savannah, causing collapses in monsoon weather patterns. The Arctic and Antarctic ice sheets could disappear altogether, releasing vast amounts of not just water into the sea but methane into the atmosphere, a gas far more potent in global-warming terms than carbon dioxide.

Fighting Dirty

The science is clear. If we carry on producing, consuming and polluting the way we are now, then it is very likely that we will cause irreparable damage to our planet, putting human societies and the natural world that sustains it in mortal danger. The solution is also remarkably clear. The United Nations' Intergovernmental Panel on Climate Change has set out a pathway to keep global warming to 1.5°C. Global net anthropogenic CO_2 emissions must decline by about 45 per cent from 2010 levels by 2030, the IPCC explains, reaching 'net zero' around 2050. This will require 'rapid and far-reaching transitions in energy, land, urban and infrastructure and industrial systems', transitions that it says are 'unprecedented in terms of scale, but not necessarily in terms of speed'.[107]

Despite the clarity of the danger and the solutions, however, many of us still have our heads buried firmly in the sand. This is understandable, as the psychological weight of this reality is hard to bear. But it is not excusable. For some, avoidance means outright denial. As Naomi Klein describes in her book, *This Changes Everything*, there is today a significant proportion of people in the global North who 'care passionately, even obsessively' about climate change, but for the wrong reasons. 'What they care about,' she says, 'is exposing it as a "hoax" being perpetrated by liberals to force them to change their light bulbs, live in Soviet-style tenements and surrender their SUVs.' For the resurgent right-wing, opposition to climate change has become 'as central to their belief system as low taxes, gun ownership and opposition to abortion'.[108]

Disturbingly, but unsurprisingly, much of this climate change denial is linked to the same ideological network of right-wing think tanks, lobbyists, journalists and politicians that we encountered in the previous chapter. Emerging just after the creation of the UN's IPCC in the late 1980s, what academics call the 'Climate Change Counter-Movement' (CCCM) operates within the same milieu as the Mont Pèlerin Society and its concentric rings of influence and power. Its aim is the same: to spread confusion and scepticism to prevent citizens and governments taking action to intervene in markets and plan the economy in the interests of society. In this case, their efforts are directed towards climate change denial, because they see that the only way to fight global warming is through state planning.[109] And the most powerful faction of the capitalist class, the fossil fuel industry, understands very well that preventing the extinction of the human race will mean extinction for them. In other words, they understand better than anyone that *climate action is class struggle*.

Researchers like Robert Brule have followed the 'dark money' behind the CCCM back to the fossil fuel corporations largely responsible for climate change in the first place. In the past, corporations like ExxonMobil were heavily involved in funding CCCM organisations through non-profit foundations and made no effort to hide it. While these corporations have apparently pulled back from funding climate change denial in the last decade or so, behind the scenes, Brule finds that it has in fact substantially increased its support through 'untraceable sources', with the US CCCM now bringing in about $900m a year.[110]

ExxonMobil provides the perfect case study of how climate change denial and 'extractivism' are fundamentally intertwined. On a corporate webpage dedicated to climate change, ExxonMobil claims that its scientists have been involved at the 'forefront of climate research for four decades, understanding and working with the world's leading experts on climate'.[111] However, as the site itself points out, the company has been at the centre of controversy – encapsulated in the Twitter hashtag #ExxonKnew – for understanding the dangers of climate change since the 1970s.

Under the umbrella of the American Petroleum Institute (API), leading fossil fuel companies – including Exxon, Texaco, as well as Standard Oil of California and Gulf Oil, the predecessors to Chevron – were initially interested in exploring alternatives to fossil fuels, not just exploring the corporate risk associated with climate change. 'API task force members appeared open to the idea that the oil industry might have to shoulder some responsibility for reducing CO_2 emissions by changing refining processes and developing fuels that emitted less carbon dioxide,' reports journalist Neela Banerjee.[112]

However, with neoliberalism becoming more and more entrenched in the 1990s, making policies such as deregulation more favourable, these fossil fuel leaders changed their approach. In 1998, just one year after the

Kyoto Protocol, a potentially game changing international treaty agreeing to cut fossil fuel emissions, the API started its first public misinformation campaign focused on undermining climate science. 'Unless "climate change" becomes a non-issue,' the API wrote in an internal memo, 'meaning that the Kyoto proposal is defeated and there are no further initiatives to thwart the threat of climate change, there may be no moment when we can declare victory for our efforts'. Later, in 2001, President George W. Bush pulled the US out of the Kyoto agreement, with another communication noting the influence of the API on Bush's decision.[113]

Exxon, of course, denies it has been fuelling climate change denial, accusing the #ExxonKnew campaigners of seeking to 'punish' the company for 'voicing its opinion on climate policy, even though the company supports policies to limit climate change'. The proof is in the pudding, however. In 2013, Exxon via its Imperial Oil subsidiary invested about $13bn to open a shale oil mine in Alberta, Canada, supplying 300,000 barrels of 'dirty oil' a day across North America. At two-hundred square kilometres – three times the size of Manhattan – this new mine has been described as the 'largest industrial project on the planet today'.[114]

Alongside other new, dirty energy investments by Chevron and Shell in Australia, we can see that fossil fuel companies have no intention of helping us meet global warming targets. 'The long timeframes attached to all these projects tell us something critical about the assumptions under which the fossil fuel industry is working,' Klein concludes. These companies have enormous amounts of capital invested in these projects, with LEX estimating that about $900bn could be wiped from the global fossil fuel industry in the IPCC's 1.5 degrees scenario.[115] These investments, therefore, show that fossil fuel giants are 'betting that governments are not going to get serious about emissions cuts for the next twenty-five to forty years'.[116] And they have the power to make sure they don't.

SWOT to Be Done

Another form of denial is the belief that someone, or something, will save us. This type of denial covers a worrying proportion of ordinary people, particularly those with comfortable, middle-class lifestyles, who would like to keep consuming as they are now. This form of consolation is leveraged by fast-moving consumer goods (FMCG) conglomerates that use 'greenwashing' techniques, such as recycled packaging, 'Fairtrade' supply chains, carbon offsetting, and so on, to convince people that it is ok to continue living in the same way, easing the guilty bourgeois conscience in exchange for premium price tags. Some take this kind of consolation even further, convincing themselves that they can bring about the climate revolution in the way that they shop.

Another variation on this theme is the idea that technology will save the world, a position that eco-Marxist John Bellamy Foster calls the 'new green Prometheanism'.[117] Microsoft co-founder and serial philanthropist Bill Gates is its personification, I would argue. In his latest book, *How to Avoid a Climate Disaster*, Gates presents the science behind climate change in clear and accessible prose, contextualising the various numbers to prevent the reader getting swamped by the scale and detail of the many individual contributing factors to global warming. Confronting the reality of climate change, Gates points out that, globally, we are adding roughly 50 billion tonnes of greenhouse gases (GHGs) to the atmosphere each year, and that keeping to 1.5 degrees will require reducing this number to as close to zero as possible, as quickly as possible.[118]

Controversially, Gates uses this 50-billion number, in true cost-benefit-calculation fashion, to dismiss many of the green alternatives favoured by the environmental movement. Reforestation, for example, as a way of removing carbon from the atmosphere is dismissed as 'overblown'. Because a typical tree absorbs on average four tons of CO_2 over a forty-year lifespan, Gates calculates that you'd need 'somewhere around 50 acres' worth of trees … to absorb the emissions produced by an average American in her lifetime'. Multiply that by the population of the United

States, he continues, and you get more than 16 billion acres, or 25 million sq. m, 'roughly half the landmass of the world'.

Divestment from fossil fuel companies is also rejected because it 'won't have a real impact on lowering emissions'. Veganism is 'not realistic' because Americans like hamburgers too much (this is Gates' stereotype, not mine) and the French are too committed to gastronomy to take sustainable living seriously. Contradicting the latest research, Gates also thinks that renewable energy – wind, solar and hydroelectric – will not get us over the line. 'The wind doesn't always blow, and the sun doesn't always shine,' he reflects, 'and we don't have affordable batteries that can store city-sized amounts of energy for long enough.'

Gates believes the solution lies in controversial alternatives like biofuels, hydrogen and nuclear power, as well as new, unproven and potentially dangerous technologies like carbon dioxide removal (CDR), in which carbon is literally sucked out of the air and put back in the ground, and geoengineering, which proposes to install mirrors in space to reflect the sun and inject sun-blocking particulates into the atmosphere. It is no coincidence that CDR is popular with the fossil fuel industry, with many experimental facilities attached to dirty energy plants. For example, after showing that it can extract CO_2 in a cost-effective way, Carbon Engineering's 'barn-sized' CDR project received $68m in investment from Chevron, Occidental and coal giant BHP.

While the fossil fuel industry sees CDR and other carbon offsetting measures as a way to maintain the status quo, Gates' interest in green high-tech comes from a different place, revealing another faction in the emerging climate class war. Gates has skin in the game, and a lot of it. 'I've put more than $1 billion into approaches that I hope will help the world get to zero,' he confesses, 'including affordable and reliable clean energy and low-emissions cement, steel, meat and more.' If you look at the list of companies that Gates' zero carbon investment vehicle, Breakthrough Energy Ventures, has invested in, it shows he has an interest in pretty much every alternative technology going.

'Lowering the Green Premiums that the world pays is not charity,' Gates argues. 'Countries like the United States shouldn't see investing in clean R&D as just a favour to the rest of the world. They should also see it as an opportunity to make scientific breakthroughs that will give birth to new industries composed of major new companies, creating jobs and reducing emissions at the same time.' In other words, the first companies to crack affordable alternatives that give a significant return on investment for finance capitalism will be the monopolists of the new green economy. Governments should encourage and support these future monopolists over fossil fuel companies because the wealth produced by them will 'trickle down' to their own citizens, and through exporting these new green technologies and the energy and sustainable products they produce, countries in the Global North can win the next phase of the imperial-capitalist war. In other words, it's just neoliberalism in new, sustainably produced clothes.

Optimism of the Intellect

Unfortunately, many leftists share, often without realising, Gates' green Prometheanism. While they may desire radically different outcomes, many share the central assumptions of this kind of tech utopianism, particularly the idea that we can carry on as we are now, as long as we 'green' production and consumption. Many on the left would, for example, agree with Gates when he says that 'the world overall should be using more of the goods and services that energy provides. There is nothing wrong with using more energy as long as it's carbon-free. The key to addressing climate change is to make clean energy just as cheap and reliable as what we get from fossil fuels.'

Many advocates for a 'Green New Deal', for example, elide the issue of whether the relations of production – that is, the fundamentally exploitative and undemocratic nature of work that creates and sustains capitalist profitability – must be transformed along with the means of production, that is, the technological and organisational apparatuses that enable commodities to be produced and consumed. First suggested by a coalition of red-green activists and experts in the UK in 2008, the Green New Deal movement calls for large-scale investment in green infrastructure and socially useful production, including naturally green industries like social care and conservation.[119]

Most Green New Deals, particularly the version proposed by US politicians Alexandria Ocasio-Cortez and Ed Markey in 2019,[120] also call for a 'just transition', which insists that people who rely on fossil fuel production and consumption for work and wealth are not made worse off by decarbonisation policies. They also put 'environmental justice' at the centre of their visions, which would address the historical and ongoing colonial and imperialist exploitation of the global South, and the suffering inflicted on 'frontline and vulnerable communities' by neoliberal public policy. However, these demands for redistribution, equality and national and international solidarity are in many cases bolted on, in the hope that, by convincing those in power that the Green New Deal is common sense, they will be able to sneak in more radical policies.

In the sense that the Green New Deal is meant to be a Trojan Horse for socialism, it represents yet another form of consolation. The reality is that any kind of real socialism, which challenges the very logic of capitalist reproduction, will need to be fought for and won through class struggle. The issue, I think, comes down to a failure to address the central contradiction in capitalist production, which has created the problem in the first place. Capitalism relies on accumulation, which, because of relentless competition between producers, must constantly expand. To stagnate is to die, and now, because of the interconnected nature of the global capitalist system, the collapse of any one of its many markets or giant companies threatens to bring the whole thing down. By its very nature, capitalism knows no limits, and has no other concern but the growth of profitability. If we accept this, then the idea of a 'sustainable capitalism' is oxymoronic.

To illustrate this problem, let's look at Kate Aronoff et al's *A Planet to Win*. Aronoff et al begin very strong, insisting on 'systemic change that tackles root causes rather than merely addressing symptoms'. They contrast a radical Green New Deal with 'faux' Green New Deals, which 'focus narrowly on swapping clean energy for fossil fuels' and see the former 'as a political liability'. Faux Green New Deals seek to achieve change by maximising elite consensus and making policy under the radar, they argue. Aronoff et al, by contrast, see the broadening of climate policy as a political asset: 'It's an opportunity to build majority support for big change and mobilize political energies to break the status quo,' they say.[121]

As with many other democratic-socialist visions of the future, the authors of *A Planet to Win* advocate genuinely radical policies that would seriously challenge capitalism's right to control production, for example, democratic, public control of 'much of the economy', with direct investment planned from above, oriented towards social use and need, and supported by thousands of community and worker-owned cooperatives operating from below. Growth for growth's sake and wealth inequality are also questioned: 'To reuse, recycle, and – most importantly – redistribute on a massive scale, a radical Green New Deal would levy higher wealth, inheritance, and upper-level income taxes to slash luxury consumption and help fund public luxuries,' they insist.

However, the fundamental question of growth or 'degrowth' – lumped together with other 'old dichotomies' on the left – is avoided. Socialism is all but named and remains the political elephant in the room: 'Contrary to the ideology of capitalism, materially intensive growth can't continue forever,' they note. 'We can't pretend ecological limits don't exist … Our view is that we need a "Last Stimulus" of green economic development in the short term to build landscapes of public affluence, develop new political-economic models, jump off the growth treadmill, break with capital, and settle into a slower groove.'

It's understandable that left-wing advocates of a Green New Deal do not want to scare off moderate readers and workers tied to polluting industries. Ultimately, a reformist green industrial revolution will need to build a broad coalition to win power and implement these policies. However, the capitalist relations of production that drive unsustainable growth and consumption are not secondary concerns that can be addressed once the policies are correctly formulated. Neither will the transition to socialism be led from above, by sections of the ruling class, nor unfold by itself out of the contradiction between extractivism and ecology. As Marx explained almost two centuries ago in *Capital*, as long as capitalism prevails, the relationships between the economy, society and nature will be exploitative and chaotic, resulting in periodic and ever more violent crises.[122]

'There is no solution to the global ecological crisis compatible with capitalist social relations,' argues Foster. 'Any ecological defences erected in the present must be based on opposition to the logic of capital accumulation. Nor can intervention by the state, acting as a kind of social capitalist, do the trick. Rather, a long ecological revolution adequate to the world's needs would mean altering the human-social metabolism with nature, countering the alienation of both nature and human labour under capitalism. Above all we must be concerned with maintaining ecological conditions for future generations – the very definition of sustainability.' I agree.[123]

Change Is Coming

A major problem with reformist strategies like the Green New Deal is that their advocates become distracted by perfecting solutions rather than helping people overcome alienation through political organisation. They convince themselves that, if they can find the right combination of radical and reasonable demands within a politically acceptable branding, they can shift the system towards socialism from the inside out. This is partly a hangover from the neoliberal era, I think, which, as we saw in the last chapter, fostered a belief that 'there is no alternative' (TINA). To counter this, the Millennial left imagines that it must first create, to twist Antonio Gramsci's phrase, an 'optimism of the intellect' before worrying about 'optimism of the will', that is, political praxis.[124]

A new generation of political activists, however, do not have this issue. Free from TINA's baggage, and not suffering from the crippling disappointment of seeing yet another attempt at parliamentary socialism fail in the US and UK (I'm referring here to Bernie Sanders and Jeremy Corbyn), these young activists are relentlessly focused on action rather 'beautiful words and promises'.[125] After going viral in 2018 when 15-year-old Greta Thunberg and others sat in front of the Swedish parliament for three weeks to protest against the lack of action on the climate crisis, the Fridays for Future movement, for example, now boasts over 14m supporters and members operating in 7,500 cities spread across the world. Key to the movement is the rediscovery of the strike weapon; every Friday, school children leave school and 'sit in front of their closest town hall, city hall or other local government building from 8am until 3pm, including holidays'.[126]

While Thunberg is keen to stress that she is not the leader of this new movement, she has become an international sensation and has used this platform to become an eloquent and powerful spokesperson for radical international climate action. In her devastating speeches to global leaders, she excoriates them for either failing to take action, or for not going far enough to meet the targets that they have themselves signed up for. For example, in her 2018 speech to the UN Climate Change Conference in Poland, she accused world leaders and 'change makers' in the audience of 'not being mature enough to tell it like it is', leaving this job instead to their children, whose future they are 'stealing'. European Union politicians have also borne the brunt of Thunberg's fury, being accused of acting like 'spoiled, irresponsible children' for 'saying everything will be alright while continuing to do nothing at all'.

Thunberg points to the corrupting influence of corporate capitalism, especially the powerful fossil fuel lobby, as one of the main barriers to radical social and economic change. 'Someone is to blame,' she insisted at the 2019 World Economic Forum meeting in Switzerland. 'Some companies and decision makers in particular,' she insisted, 'have known exactly what priceless values they are sacrificing to continue making unimaginable amounts of money.' This essentially class-based analysis is crucial, she insisted, because 'if everyone is guilty then no one is to blame' – a kind of consolation that is 'just another convenient lie'.

While the Fridays for Future movement has no plan for replacing capitalism – it is not interested in clever policies, as already noted – what distinguishes Thunberg from Green New Dealers is a clarity of focus, with unequivocal language shifting the responsibility for fighting climate change consistently back to the politicians who, if they worked together and were true to their warm words, would have the power to take on the fossil fuel industry and make the kinds of massive public investments necessary. 'There are no grey areas when it comes to survival,' she maintains.

It is also important to situate the Fridays for Future movement within a longer history of environmentalism that is not only increasingly driven by young people, but also by young people of colour and of indigenous origin. Thunberg herself notes the influence of Zero Hour, a US-based youth-led climate action organisation founded by Jamie Margolin. Like Thunberg, Margolin – who describes herself as being a first-generation daughter of a 'Latina immigrant from Columbia'[127] – was driven to action by the 'existential threat' of climate change. Since founding Zero Hour, Margolin has sued the state of Washington for denying young people their 'constitutional rights to life, liberty and the pursuit of happiness by actively worsening the climate crisis.'[128] She organised the international climate march in 2018 that inspired Thunberg to strike a month later, and later testified in front of US Congress alongside Thunberg about the impacts of climate change on her generation.[129]

However, it was arguably the Dakota Access Pipeline protests that crystallised the international youth climate movement we see today. In 2014, Energy Transfer Partners announced plans to build an 1,886 km underground oil pipeline stretching from a shale oil field in North Dakota to a refinery in Illinois, which would run straight through Standing Rock Sioux territory and underneath a key tribal resource. In response, members of the Missouri River tribe led by LaDonna Brave Bull Allard and the International Indigenous Youth Council (IIYC) created the Sacred Stone Camp and began a programme of civil disobedience aimed at stopping the construction of the pipeline.

At its height in 2016, the Sacred Stone Camp attracted youth activists from across the world, including Margolin and future US Congresswoman and Green New Deal advocate Alexandria Ocasio-Cortez. Their non-violent protests – which included Standing Rock youth aged 6 to 25 running 2,000 miles to Washington DC to deliver a 160,000 strong petition opposing the pipeline to President Obama – resulted in construction being paused. Unfortunately, one of the first things that Donald Trump did when he became president in 2017 was to sign an executive order allowing construction to resume.[130] Despite his grand promises to

improve tribal relations and initiate long-term action to tackle climate
change, new president Biden has, at the time of writing, so far made no
indication he will stop construction of the pipeline.[131]

Socialism or Barbarism

Like many international social movements, Fridays for Future was
forced to scale back activities during the pandemic. But we should not
understate the impact this movement has had on global climate action.
It is certainly the case that corporations and their representatives in capitalist democratic states have responded mostly with rebranding and
a realisation that the pandemic represents an historic opportunity to
'pivot' towards the green economy. It is also true that the desire for a
more sustainable way of living among ordinary people lasted only for
the briefest moment before hyper-consumption resumed during second,
third and fourth lockdowns.

   However, we need to see this struggle as one that will take place over
the period of an entire generation. Even if I live a long and healthy life,
I will probably only just see how the fate of the planet is decided, I will not
be there to build the new world if we win. It is right that we must focus
a lot of energy on accelerating climate action to keep global warming to
an absolute minimum. But we must also put as much energy as we can
into building the institutions and movements capable of changing the
system for good. Because if we let neoliberalism recycle itself, we will
only stumble into yet another crisis down the line.

   To be pessimistic, which is not really my style, if we don't bring radical change, we will see unprecedented global political chaos. Millions of
people across the world are already trying to escape the effects of global
warming ~ floods, droughts, extreme weather, sea level rises, biodiversity
loss. Even citizens of wealthier countries are starting to see these impacts
first hand, and with wave upon wave of migration hitting their borders
over the next few years, more so if there are military conflicts over natural
resources, they will become increasingly fearful. This fear will be mobilised

by the far right, and by reactionary political parties desperate to cling onto power. The point is not to scare you. The point is to emphasise that inaction is, in this context, inexcusable.

People are scared. I'm scared. Climate change is overwhelming, as is starting out on the path towards the alternative. But we can do it, together.

While young activists got stuck in endless debates about whether to try and shift centre-left parties further to the left, or start new red-green parties from scratch, many older left-wing intellectuals had given up trying to change the world entirely. A new generation of Marxist academics – many having established themselves in the Corbyn era with 'prefigurative' plans that now seemed more than utopian – had either buried themselves in theory or made a career out of repeating the same argument about the imminent collapse of neoliberalism (this time, this time!). But the academy was far from the refuge they had dreamed of while labouring through their Ph. D theses. Many universities were now teaching factories, with precariously employed young academics in for-profit subsidiary companies delivering bite-sized packets of learning via MOOCs – Massive Open Online Courses. There were still a few pseudo-tenured jobs in the charitable parent institutions – retained for branding purposes – but these were incredibly hard to get. Only the most entrepreneurial and competitive star academics got these jobs and retained them only at huge personal cost.

Aisha had been one of these idealistic young scholars, having grown up in a nice middle-class family, with university educated parents, surrounded by books and culture. Going to university was an obvious choice, as was doing a Master's and a PhD, especially given the state of the job market after the pandemic. But after toiling away as an hourly paid Sociology 'tutor' for a couple of years with no hope of promotion or future job security, she became a University and College Union rep, and became increasingly politicised. She helped unionise her subsidiary, winning some improvements to colleagues' terms and conditions along the way. She also helped to unionise outsourced cleaners and porters, realising that many academics now shared similar conditions to the most badly treated yet invisible sections of the university work force. Aisha's relentless organising and inspirational determination made her a legend in the labour movement, and she is now standing to become UCU's first Black female President (this would have been Nita Sanghera, who died tragically in 2020).

'It's time to make a stand against neoliberalism, not just in education, but in society generally,' opens Aisha's UCU election manifesto. 'For decades, we've let corporations and speculators, and their government representatives, hollow out our public services and destroy the hopes and dreams of

our children. We've stood by while they've gutted the earth and annihilated species and natural ecosystems. We can't just defend our own interests any longer. Within tertiary education, our teaching conditions are our students' learning conditions. We must stand with students and our colleagues in administration and facilities and reclaim our schools, colleges, universities and other education institutions for the common good. We must also recognise ourselves as workers, currently producing value for a new class of managers and bosses, just like workers in any other industry or sector. We need to transform the meaning of value in society into something social, something ecological. And we can only do that side by side with our comrades; with the millions of unemployed and underemployed thrown in and out of work by this broken system; and with our communities devastated by not just one crisis, but by the constant crisis that is capitalism.'

CHAPTER 4

We Are Fighting for Everyone's Future

Once upon a time, universities were sanctuaries for higher learning and intellectual inquiry. Students and academics enjoyed the freedom to explore whatever topics were of interest to them, within a general framework of humanistic culture. Nation states saw the intrinsic value of higher education, and by extension, the universities in which such education took place, and therefore funded this community of scholars without any strings attached. The material basis for this freedom was protected by tenure, which guaranteed an internationally recognised professoriate a secure and well-paid life, and significant say over university governance, after an early career apprenticeship filled with insecurity and intellectual competition – a rite of passage for every academic.

Then came along the big bad wolf of neoliberal capitalism, which wanted to blow down the walls of this ivory tower to bring universities in line with the globalised, financialised economy. Students were to become consumers of higher education, and academics merely providers of this service, much like a Starbucks barista provides cappuccino after cappuccino to an endless line of coffee-hungry commuters. The analogy works well, as students in this model are 'entrepreneurs of the self', investing in their own 'human capital' to gain competitive advantage in the world of graduate work.[132] A degree is merely a stop off point on the conveyor belt of birth, work, consumerism and death.

This is the story that most academics tell themselves today, working under relentless pressure to teach and mark coursework from an ever-expanding student body, while researching when they can, often in evenings, weekends or on annual leave. Beleaguered by marketisation, these scholars console themselves with an ideal past of academic life, in some cases, constructing whole philosophical theories of the 'public university' in the hope that policy makers will read their numerous books and reconsider their evil plans. Of course, they don't.

As always, the past is more complicated. Academic freedom, a concept now held up as an eternal value, was in fact won through collective action and political struggle. European universities started out as an unexceptional kind of medieval guild, in this case an association of 'Masters' or students (or both) seeking to teach or learn the knowledge needed to access good jobs in local government or in the Catholic church. The 'universitas' structure was adopted to protect the material interests of these scholarly communities against the kings and emperors that wanted to use them for their own political or economic purposes.

In the thirteenth century, for example, academics at the University of Paris went on strike, after the over-zealous local authority killed a group of innocent students because of a local bar brawl. Finding their strike ineffective, the Masters resorted to the nuclear option: 'secession'. They dissolved the university for a period of six years and left Paris. Some went to England at the invitation of Henry III, reinforcing the rising universities of Oxford and Cambridge. Others seceded to smaller 'studium generale' or cathedral schools of France: Toulouse, Orleans, Reims and Angers, where universities were eventually established as a result.[133]

Thanks to the secession, the Masters, who eventually returned to the University of Paris, were granted the right to make their own statutes by the Papal authorities, an important element of the self-governance that underpinned academic freedom for centuries after. What this struggle shows is not only that academic freedom was won through collective action, but also that academics have had to be strategic when picking their political and material allies. While in many cases, Masters sided with students to protect their shared interests, they also gambled on the Church maintaining its authority over the emerging national states – a bet that was far from sure at the time.

Elsewhere, students sometimes had to act against their Masters. While Paris was formed by academics and backed by the Pope, the University of Bologna established itself as a student-led community against the interests of academics, who they feared would, at a pinch, side with the municipal authorities over them. Instead of waiting for such a situation to arise, the students at the end of the twelfth century took the initiative, appointing themselves a universitas scolarium, which, through student-led militancy, managed to impose its will on the Masters.[134]

What the history of the university tells us, then, is that academic freedom is not something like a philosophy or 'soul' of the university that precedes or transcends its history. It is a collective achievement that has been won through organisation and struggle. As we will see in the next section, this achievement has had to be defended repeatedly, and as already noted, is once again under attack. As in the past, academics must today choose their allies wisely.

Philosopher Kings

By the end of the eighteenth century, the fate of the European university, which had proven to be a surprisingly enduring medieval institution, was in question. In 1793, at the height of the French Revolution, the National Convention – the revolutionary parliament – abolished the twenty-two universities operating at the time, including the University of Paris. While universities gradually began to reappear in the nineteenth century under Napoleon Bonaparte, fully modernised and headed by the state-controlled University of France, the terror of both revolution and university abolition provoked heated debate across Europe about the future of higher education.[135]

Nowhere more so than across the border, in Germany, particularly among a small group of scholars promoting a new kind of philosophy: German Idealism. And it was the father of German Idealism, Immanuel Kant, that made the first move in a hugely influential article, 'The Conflict of the Faculties'. In this essay Kant argues that the Faculty of Philosophy (i.e. the Arts and Humanities) is much better qualified, as the only Faculty concerned solely with truth and invested with the authority of pure reason, to lead the university.

Setting a precedent for subsequent attempts to reform, rather than revolutionise, the medieval university, and protect the social and material position of scholars in the process, Kant finishes the essay with a pitch to the new King of Prussia, Frederick William III. Kant advocates not only a reversal of power between Faculties, shifting power away from the supposedly 'higher' faculties, Theology, Law and Medicine, but also that the government should heed the relentless criticism of philosophers. 'For the new German government may find the freedom of philosophy proposed here and the increased insight gained from this freedom a better means for achieving its ends than its own absolute authority,' he writes.[136]

Amazingly, the government listened, or at least Prussian official Wilhelm von Humboldt did. At von Humboldt's suggestion, the King founded the University of Berlin in 1808. While this new university might not have matched the lofty ideas of the idealist philosophers who provided its ideology, it established many enduring structures that would provide the export model for universities across the world. 'It fused together a reshaping of the traditional university form,' explains university historian Robert Anderson. 'An ideal of scholarship in which teaching and research fructified each other, a set of academic practices which were held to guarantee academic freedom, a new relationship with the state, and a neohumanist ethos which bound universities and secondary schools.'[137]

It is this model that most academics explicitly or implicitly refer to in their defences of the 'public university'. It is no coincidence that Kant also provides us with the idea of the 'public sphere', which takes the university as its institutional ideal. For Kant, modern science, backed by his own critical philosophy, provides people with the tools to liberate themselves from ignorance. 'Dare to know!' he urges the readers of his famous essay, 'What is Enlightenment?' 'Have the courage to use your own intelligence.'[138]

However, while Kant's critical philosophy, in principle, allowed for anyone to liberate themselves from ignorance through inquiry, in reality, he considered that philosophers would be the most courageous when it came to this challenge, and, as a result, should be tasked with educating the ignorant masses through the dissemination of the critical knowledge they had discovered. 'It is difficult for the isolated individual to work himself out of the immaturity which has become almost natural for him,' he points out. 'But it is more nearly possible for a public to enlighten itself.'[139]

The university, then, was to be the means for this public Enlightenment. With Kant's theory of the public university, we have the archetype of the 'bourgeois' public sphere: formally democratic but materially circumscribed by wealth, status or, in the capitalist era, the ability to secure the necessary social and/or cultural capital to access the 'best' institutions of education that in turn open the doors to the establishment elite.[140] We also have in Kant the clearest expression of the bargain offered by intellectuals to the German authorities: secure our material existence and we will provide you with the human capital and R&D ('useful' research and development) needed for the rapid creation of a capitalist state.

This is not just a fascinating history. The modern university perfectly expresses the central contradiction in capitalist societies between democracy and the reality of capitalist reproduction. On the one hand, democracy provides the capitalist system with political legitimacy. It provides formal rights that, in principle, allow everyone to flourish and hold governments to account. However, the relations of production shape how these rights are distributed and used in practice.

Most people have little wealth or power, while a minority have both. Inherited wealth still gives many people a significant head-start in life, along with the social and cultural capital that greases the wheels of meritocracy.[141] But it is the legalised exploitation at the heart of this system, where most people have no choice but to work to live, while a minority have the right to steal a proportion of people's labour for their own profit, which funnels wealth and power always upwards. As we saw in Chapter 1, education, particularly higher education, acts to hide the reality of these relations of production. The failure of most working-class people to thrive in formal education settings proves that they shouldn't have been there in the first place.

Human Capital

For many British academics, the 1963 Robbins Report represents a watershed moment in the history of public higher education. While this is true to a certain extent, the report, as we will see, also expresses quite clearly the contradiction described above. At its core is the now famous axiom that courses of higher education 'should be available for all those who are qualified by ability and attainment to pursue them and who wish to do so'.[142] For British sociologist John Holmwood – a vocal critic of marketisation in the UK, who formed the Campaign for the Public University in 2011 – this was a 'clear endorsement of a social democratic view of education'.[143]

Holmwood also argues that the four aims of higher education as described by the report – instruction in skills; the promotion of general powers of the mind; the advancement of learning; and the transmission of a common culture and common standards of citizenship – taken together with a general commitment to equality of opportunity, represent a shift towards the idea of 'social rights', which are substantive rights that people must have access to for democracy to function properly.

Here Holmwood is referring to an argument made by British post-war sociologist T. H. Marshall. In his influential 1949 essay 'Citizenship and Social Class', Marshall argues that social democracy constituted the endpoint of a long process of democratisation, with the British welfare state ensuring that every citizen (with citizenship linked to the national state) had the 'right to a modicum of social welfare and security' and a right to 'share to the full in the social heritage and to live the life of a civilised being according to the standards prevailing in the society'.[144]

With its commitment to free education for all those who pass the relevant exams, with fees paid by the state and students supported by taxpayer-funded grants, the era following Robbins was indeed a high point for public higher education. For Robbins, however, it wasn't Marshall that provided the ideological justification for such radical investment in education, but a new, controversial idea in neoliberal economics: 'Human Capital Theory'.

Human Capital Theory (HCT) was first introduced in the early 1960s by Chicago School economist Theodor Schultz to expand the idea of fixed capital investment – where firms invest in technology to increase the productivity of the labour process – to include human beings. According to Schultz, economic growth 'depends not only on the nation's physical capital (such as roads), but also on the education and health of the labour pool'.[145] Schultz asserted that the 'rates of return on such human capital investment are greater than those for nonhuman capital investments, and that any short-term losses incurred as a result of time taken out of careers for education or money invested in health care are acceptable risks as they produce greater long-term economic and social gains for both individual and society'.[146]

For Robbins, himself a highly respected economist and member of the Mont Pèlerin Society, the puzzle was how to create a system that captured both the private and the social benefits of higher education. A 'fundamental difficulty', he noted, was that the return on education, 'even if it be considered solely in terms of productivity, is not something that can be estimated completely in terms of the return to individuals and of differential earnings'.[147] So, Robbins and his colleagues had to be content with abstract arguments for the socio-economic value of free higher education to justify the massive public investment they were proposing.

Jumping forward in time to the post-Financial Crisis era, former UK universities minister David Willetts didn't see himself, with his ambitious plans to introduce a market into the English higher education system, as destroyer of public higher education, but rather the completer of Robbins' revolution. Specifically, he considered himself to have solved the report's 'fundamental difficulty' through the income-contingent loan (ICL) system. Essentially ICLs act like a graduate tax in which repayments are only made once wages reach a minimum level set by policy makers. Depending on the level this minimum threshold is set, a certain proportion of loans never get repaid.

Critics of marketisation have made much of the non-repayment of loans, insisting that it showed that the system didn't work. But for Willetts, the fact that roughly half of loans would be written off, becoming the responsibility of the taxpayer, represents accurately the ratio of value represented by higher education. 'Higher education brings a mixture of private and public gain so you could argue that it makes sense to fund it out of a mix of payment by the graduate beneficiaries and the Exchequer,' Willetts explains in his memoir, *A University Education*.[148] The Tory-Liberal Democrat coalition government estimated it was 'broadly shifting the balance of funding from 60:40 public/private to 40:60,' he says, which is 'not far from some of the historic estimates of private and public gains'.

Furthermore, the information generated by student loans, combined with existing labour force data, would allow a government to calculate the return on investment for higher education, for both taxpayer and individuals. Once enough data is generated, institutions and even courses can be rated according to their economic benefit, specifically what kind of wages graduates can expect from say an arts and humanities degree versus one in the area of science or engineering. Ignoring completely the laws of cause and effect, in which the demand for skilled labour is determined by investment in real productivity, neoliberals imagine that more science and engineering graduates will boost the ailing, financialised economy.

As Andrew McGettigan argues, this kind of big data neoliberalism – which is supported in the area of R&D production by the Research Excellence and Knowledge Exchange Frameworks – allows higher education to be conceptualised as 'variable human capital investment', which is to say as a private investment by individuals in future economic prosperity and an arm's length government system for managing economic productivity. Individuals and institutions are rewarded or punished according to how wisely they invest; education is reduced to cost-benefit analysis.[149] Here we come full circle. We see yet another attempt by neoliberalism to 'nudge' people into behaving more economically.

Ecological Universities

Today, then, academic freedom is once again under attack. So, what should we do about it? As described in the last chapter, humanity is facing the biggest and most serious challenge it has perhaps ever faced in the form of climate change. The one thing we cannot afford to do is pretend that higher education exists in a bubble, that academic freedom must be defended against all kinds of attack, including from those rightly demanding the democratisation of knowledge. As explained above, academics have historically been very savvy about protecting their material interests. They have chosen their allies carefully and have managed to ensure the ongoing existence of the university as one of the oldest public institutions. Today, they must again choose sides. And, as in the past, I think they should once again choose to stand with youth.

The solution to climate change is also the solution to the problem of higher education, and, in fact, the economic crisis as a whole. As the IPCC said, keeping global warming to 1.5 degrees will require 'unprecedented … rapid and far-reaching transitions in energy, land, urban and infrastructure and industrial systems'. True, in making this rapid transition, many jobs would become obsolete, for example, in the fossil fuel or fossil-fuel-adjacent industries. But a 'just transition' would make sure that people are retrained for new, good, green jobs.[150] These jobs would have a wider social meaning as well, providing people with an opportunity to feel less alienated in their work life, and therefore more engaged as citizens of the world.[151]

Radical climate action would also potentially transform the meaning of tertiary education, dis-alienating in particular academic labour, which has historically kept itself at a distance from social concerns. In my own work, I have tried to develop a model of socially useful, ecological universities, which would become hubs for the kind of collective intelligence outlined in this book and in *The Method of Democracy*.[152] University workers and students could work directly with local communities, looking at how their needs can be served by socially useful, human-centred technologies. Working closely with schools and colleges, ecological universities could also become relays for a revitalised democracy, building a new world from the bottom up.

Something amazing started happening towards the end of the decade. Countless community groups and grassroots political organisations came together to create a network of mutual aid, solidarity, communication and, eventually, strategic co-operation. No single individual or group led the way, people just started to realise that, unless they built something together, they were never going to defeat the far right and force international action on climate change. Trade unions and red-green community alliances created local 'combines' – structures able to work across artificial divides – and win key battles on issues like housing, transport and food. Together, these combines formed new inter-regional democratic institutions to influence national politics, electing a new wave of radical Labour and Green Party MPs that were serious about changing the world.

Many universities and colleges were now in constant occupation, with an army of students and workers ready to pile into any strike, irrespective of reactionary trade union legislation. These strikes and occupations also became centres of radical democracy, working closely with the combine movement to coordinate local and regional action. While all this was happening, the education sector essentially ground to a halt. But parents didn't mind, because the movement also built an alternative education network, centred on the principles and practices of 'critical pedagogy'. On picket lines and in repurposed retail units, striking teachers, occupying students and residents learned from each other as human beings, beginning with the realities of life and working out from there to massive issues facing humankind and the natural world.

No one could have seen this happening just a few years ago, in the wake of the pandemic. But collective intelligence never dies. It sometimes goes underground, kept alive by the hardcore, finding new struggles to feed on while the objective conditions remain hostile. Like flowering bulbs, collective intelligence lies patiently during long, cold winters until the first rays of sun warm the ground, indicating that the time has come to burst through the soil and unleash a wave of irresistible beauty to cover the earth. The insects and bees – the workers of the natural world – then swarm to these flowers, nourishing themselves and their communities so they will thrive for another season. We must never give up hope in collective intelligence. We must always find the energy to bloom together again.

Conclusion: There Are No Grey Areas When It Comes to Survival

Change is coming, whether we like it or not. As well as being one of Greta's best lines, it is also one of the key messages of this book. Change is coming from young people like Greta, who have only a bleak future ahead of them, and are sick of politicians lying to them for their own benefit and in the interests of other, already rich and powerful adults. As explained in Chapter 1, young people see through the false promises of education, with which they must engage if they are to get a decent job (or a job at all). They are cynical, but also smarter than ever; tech savvy, ready to use the tools they have to drive change. What sort of change do young people want? This is still an open question, and one that we, adults, parents, educators, comrades and citizens must attend to if we are to be part of this change. We are not here to take over, but rather to listen, to share our wisdom and help.

Young people are only responding to the conditions they have inherited. Climate change, structural under-employment, pandemics – these are all effects that can be ultimately traced back to the irrationality of the capitalist system. Another key message of the book is that change – and chaos – are the very essence of the capitalist system. Change is the condition of its survival. Without relentless, chaotic transformation, capitalism will defeat itself. Monopolies will take over the world and kill competition once and for all. Even the alienated forms of political and social freedom we have will die. Capitalism will become its own nightmare – 'totalitarianism', a system it ideologically associates with socialism, but which is, in fact, its own logical conclusion.

This constant renewal is reflected, and in part driven by, capitalist ideology. Chapter 2 traced the reinvention of neoliberalism as 'libertarian paternalism'. A bizarre kind of non-interventionist state intervention, conservative governments now manipulate us through 'nudges' into becoming the perfect producers and consumers of an imperfect capitalist system. But this is only a waystation on the long journey of ideological reinvention, serving merely as a case study. Neoliberalism is not dying and will not of its own accord – another core message, one that the left never seems to hear. This liberal paternalism indicates a warmer embrace of the state, already present in neoliberal governance, and a willingness to dispense with democracy in favour of economic reproduction.

Crisis, even unprecedentedly disruptive ones like the 2008 Financial Crisis or the coronavirus pandemic, are potentially progressive, from capital's point of view. Economic crises reset production. They eliminate unproductive capital and provide new investment opportunities for the survivors. Between these eternally recurring busts, the heroes of neoliberal capitalism – the entrepreneurs – hound the monopolists, searching out their weaknesses, inventing new weapons of 'disruption' to kill them off and take their place. Meanwhile, the vultures of finance pick the corpses. The short sellers hedge their bets, backing the disruptors as well as betting on their failure – sometimes, as in the case of Michael Burry, on the failure of the entire system.

Even climate change – perhaps the most serious crisis humankind has ever faced – is just another investment opportunity. This is another message I wanted to stress with this book. As Chapter 3 showed, the reactionary wing of the capitalist class – the fossil fuel industry and its hedge fund investors and carbon speculators – will hold out for as long as possible, squeezing out as much profit as they can before jumping ship and claiming good will. They may even embrace fascism to protect their material interests. Meanwhile, the more progressive factions of international capital have already accepted the inevitable and are making moves to capture market share in the new green economy. Some of this is 'greenwashing', of course. But some of it is genuine. Profit is capital's only religion; all other beliefs can be easily jettisoned.

This war within the capitalist ruling class is already being waged and is being represented at the level of the state. Democratic governments have a tough job today. They must somehow balance and further the interests of international and national capital, the dirty and the clean players, while maintaining hegemony at home. Periods of crisis, however, highlight and exacerbate the inequality, corruption and stagnation that is always present in capitalism, but is hidden by consumerism and distraction. As the collapse of hegemony becomes more acute, and bribery becomes less and less affordable, governments may opt out of democracy, with disastrous results.

We have already seen how dog-whistle politics and fearmongering have shifted mainstream parties far to the right. In the UK, the 2016 EU referendum dragged the entire country into an internal war within the Conservative Party, dividing the country into Leavers and Remainers and boosting British neo-fascism. Representing the reactionary wing of the Tory Party, Boris Johnson used the victory of Leave to win the 2019 election, running on a Trumpian platform of 'making Britain great again'. His party's vision is now one of pure neoliberalism. Behind the big coronavirus spending, his secretaries of state are turning the UK into a deregulated free market utopia, with a nation of low-paid workers and destitute communities kept in line by increasingly authoritarian policing laws.

In the US, by contrast, Joe Biden represents the progressive wing of international capital. He wants to rebuild America through investment in infrastructure and a just transition. However, despite running on a radical platform, cashing in on the base built by the Democratic Socialists of America, this is not a socialist Green New Deal. It is, rather, an investment vehicle for the new green capitalism. Nevertheless, it is better than fascism, and Trump is waiting just round the corner to pounce if Biden fails. In one sense, the fate of the planet lies with the US. A progressive America would do much to repair the foundations of Western capitalism, helping it stumble along to the next crisis. A fascist one would massively boost the international far right, halt and even reverse progress on global warming and plunge the globe into further chaos.

The contrast between these two possible futures is stark. But there is another. Even in the most beleaguered parts of society, collective intelligence remains ready to flower. In the youthful climate change movement, out of the struggles over public education, there is potential for renewal. As suggested in Chapter 4, if education workers can rediscover their collective power, unite with students and communities around shared material concerns, a new set of democratic institutions could be built to nurture and politicise collective intelligence. It's true, right now, this model seems utopian. I seem to be committing to another form of 'consolation'. But as Dewey always said, we need an 'end-in-view' to guide action. And I'm not just writing books, I'm out there with others, fighting to make this vision, or something like it, a reality.

If there's is one message, then, that I'd like you to take away from this book, it's that hope must be matched by action if we are to avoid consolation. We cannot afford to be distracted by wishful thinking, or be manipulated by those that would use our legitimate fears against us. The earth is dying, and politically, things can get a lot, lot worse. But if it takes five or even ten years to build an effective movement that can beat neoliberalism and neo-fascism, that's better than creating something quickly that will lose. The key is to win, and to win we must be smart, we must be brave and more than anything, we must act together.

Notes

Preface: Blah Blah Blah

1 World Health Organization Coronavirus (COVID-19) Dashboard, 20 April 2021: <https://covid19.who.int/>. The number of deaths as a result of the coronavirus pandemic is itself a deeply controversial subject, with conspiracy theorists (most famously, Donald Trump) claiming a much lower number, and others claiming the opposite. Interestingly, the WHO itself has criticised governments for under-reporting the number of direct and indirect deaths from SARS-CoV-2 in 2020 and 2021, putting the figure closer to 15m worldwide. https://www.bmj.com/content/377/bmj.o1144 [Last accessed 28 July 2022].

2 International Labour Organization (2021) ILO Monitor: COVID-19 and the World of Work. Seventh edition: <https://www.ilo.org/global/topics/coronavirus/impacts-and-responses/WCMS_767028/lang--en/index.htm> [Last accessed 28 July 2022].

3 UNICEF, 17 September 2021: <https://www.unicef.org/press-releases/schoolchildren-worldwide-have-lost-1.8-trillion-hours-and-counting-person-learning> [Last accessed 28 July 2022].

4 ILO (2021) Briefing Note, 'An Update on the Youth Labour MARKET impact of the COVID-19 Crisis': <https://www.ilo.org/emppolicy/pubs/WCMS_795479/lang--en/index.htm> [Last accessed 28 July 2022].

5 Greta Thunberg's speech at the Youth4Climate 'Driving Ambition' Pre-COP26 event. Video available on Thunber's Twitter feed: <https://twitter.com/GretaThunberg/status/1442860615941468161> [Last accessed 20 April 2022].

6 See, for example, the excellent analyses of the impact of the coronavirus in China by the heterodox Marxist group Chuang, published in the book *Social Contagion,* for a summary of the research on the origins of COVID-19 in the contradictions of the global capitalist economy: <https://chuangcn.org/books/social-contagion/> [Last accessed 28 July 2022].

7 John Dewey diagnosed consolation in theory as the search for a 'feeling of certainty' in the 'absence of actual certainty in the midst of a precarious and hazardous world' – see, for example, Dewey, J. (1998) 'Philosophy's Search for the Immutable', in Hickman, L. A. and Alexander, T. M. (eds), *The Essential Dewey, Volume 1: Pragmatism, Education, Democracy.* Bloomington: Indiana University Press, p. 105.

8   'My propositions are elucidatory in this way: he who understands me finally
        recognizes them as senseless, when he has climbed out through them, on them,
        over them. (He must so to speak throw away the ladder, after he has climbed
        up on it.) He must surmount these propositions; then he sees the world rightly.'
        Wittgenstein, L. (1922) *Tractatus Logico-Philosophicus*. London: Routledge,
        p. 90 (§ 6.54)
9   Peterson, J. (1999) *Maps of Meaning: The Architecture of Belief*. London: Routledge.
10   Fisher, M. (2009) *Capitalist Realism: Is There No Alternative?* London: Zero Books.

Change Is Coming Whether You Like It or Not

11   See Bourdieu, P. and Passeron, J.-C. (1979) *The Inheritors: French Students and
        Their Relation to Culture*. Chicago: University of Chicago Press and Bourdieu,
        P. and Passeron, J.-C. (1990) *Reproduction in Education, Society and Culture*.
        London: SAGE.
12   See, for example, Rancière, J. (2004) *The Philosopher and his Poor*. Durham: Duke
        University
        Press and Rancière, J. (2012) *Proletarian Nights: The Workers Dream in 19th
        Century France*. London:
        Verso.
13   Rancière, J. (2012) 'The Ethics of Sociology', in *The Intellectual and His
        People: Staging the People Volume 2*. London: Verso, p. 162.
14   Gramsci, A. (1971) *Selections from the Prison Notebooks of Antonio Gramsci*.
        London: Lawrence & Wishart
15   Schwartzmantel, J. (2015) *The Routledge Guidebook to Gramsci's Prison Notebooks*.
        London: Routledge, p. 76
16   Pelletier, C. (2009) 'Emancipation, Equality and Education: Rancière's Critique
        of Bourdieu and the Question of Performativity'. *Discourse: Studies in the
        Cultural Politics of Education* 30 (2), pp. 137-50.
17   Rancière, J. (2012) 'The Ethics of Sociology', in *The Intellectual and His
        People: Staging the People Volume 2*. London: Verso, p. 162
18   'Someone once said that it is easier to imagine the end of the world than to im-
        agine the end of capitalism' – Fredric Jameson (2003) 'Future City'. *New Left
        Review*   21(3):   <https://newleftreview.org/issues/ii21/articles/fredric-jame
        son-future-city> - here Jameson is actually quoting himself in an earlier book,
        The Seeds of Time. The quote has an interesting history. According to Matthew
        Beaumont, Jameson is 'probably misremembering some comments made by
        H. Bruce Franklin about J. G. Ballard, "that it is easier to imagine the end of

the world than to imagine the end of capitalism". See Beaumont, M. (2014) 'Imagining the End Times: Ideology, the Contemporary Disaster Movie, Contagion' in Flisfeder, M. and Willis, L. P. (eds), *Žižek and Media Studies*. New York: Palgrave Macmillan.

19   'TINA' is phrase used repeatedly by Thatcher in her speeches – see *The Independent* (8 April 2013) <https://www.independent.co.uk/news/uk/polit ics/margaret-thatcher-her-own-words-8564762.html> and for Fukuyama, see his 1989 article, 'The End of History?' in the *The National Interest* (16: 3-18 – Accessed 22 May 2021), which you can find here: <http://www.jstor.org/stable/ 24027184>.

20   Bourdieu, P. and Passeron, J.-C. (1979) *The Inheritors: French Students and Their Relation to Culture*. Chicago: University of Chicago Press, p. 84.

21   Marx, K. (1999) *Capital: A Critique of Political Economy, Volume I* – Part V: The Production of Absolute and of Relative Surplus-Value. [Online] <https://www. marxists.org/archive/marx/works/1867-c1/ch16.htm> [Last accessed 28 July 2022].

22   Bourdieu and Passeron (1979), p. 83.

23   Ibid, pp. 84-5.

24   See Kristin Ross' excellent 2002 book, *May '68 and Its Afterlives*. Chicago: Chicago University Press, and also the introduction to mine and Stephen Cowden's 2019 edited collection, *The Practice of Equality: Jacques Rancière and Critical Pedagogy*. Oxford: Peter Lang.

25   Ainley, P. (2016) *Betraying a Generation: How Education is Failing Young People*. Bristol: Policy Press, p. 38.

26   Ibid, p. 36.

27   Office for National Statistics (ONS) (2016). 'Unemployment' [Online]. Available from: <https://www.ons.gov.uk/employmentandlabourmarket/peoplenotinwork/ unemployment> [Last accessed 28 July 2022] – see also Ridley, D. (2020) *The Method of Democracy*, p. 60.

28   Referenced by Ainley (2016), on p. 33.

29   Ibid, p. 17.

30   Ibid.

31   Ibid, p. 89.

32   Ibid, p. 2.

33   Gardiner et al. (2020) *An intergenerational audit for the UK* [Online]: <https:// www.resolutionfoundation.org/publications/intergenerational-audit-uk-2020/> [Last accessed 28 July 2022].

34   Joseph Rowntree Foundation (2021) *UK Poverty 2020/21* [Online]: <https:// www.jrf.org.uk/report/uk-poverty-2020-21> [Last accessed 28 July 2022].

35   Gardiner et al. (2020), p. 10.

36   <https://www.theguardian.com/society/2020/oct/07/covid-generation-uk-youth-unemployment-set-to-triple-to-80s-levels> [Last accessed 28 July 2022].

37   Office for National Statistics (2021) 'Youth Unemployment, January to March 2019 to October to December 2020' [Use requested data]: <https://www.ons. gov.uk/employmentandlabourmarket/peoplenotinwork/unemployment/adh ocs/12960youthunemploymentjanuarytomarch2019tooctobertodecember2 020> [Accessed 22 May 2021].

38   Ibid.

39   Gardiner et al. (2020), p. 56.

40   Ibid, p. 59.

41   Ibid, p. 43.

42   Ibid, p. 59.

43   In her first speech as leader of the Conservative Party in 1975, Thatcher said she was following in the footsteps of Anthony Eden in pursuing the goal of a 'property-owning democracy' in Britain: <https://www.margaretthatcher.org/ document/102777> [Last accessed 28 July 2022].

44   Gardiner et al. (2020), p. 68.

45   Joseph Rowntree Foundation, p. 75.

46   Ibid, p. 56.

47   Ibid.

48   Ibid, p. 24.

49   World Economic Forum (2021) The Global Risks Report: 16th Edition [Online]:<https://www.weforum.org/reports/the-global-risks-report-2021>[Last accessed 28 July 2022].

50   Ibid, p. 44.

51   Ibid, p. 40.

52   Ibid, p. 42.

53   Ibid.

54   BBC News (13 November 2020) 'US Election 2020: Results and Exit Poll in Maps and Charts' [Online]: <https://www.bbc.co.uk/news/election-us-2020-54783016> [Last accessed 28 July 2022].

55   Moore, P. (2016) 'How Britain Voted at the EU Referendum' [Online]: <https:// yougov.co.uk/topics/politics/articles-reports/2016/06/27/how-britain-voted> [Last accessed 28 July 2022].

56   McDonnell, A. and Curtis, C. (2019) 'How Britain Voted in the 2019 General Election' [Online]:<https://yougov.co.uk/topics/politics/articles-reports/2019/ 12/17/how-britain-voted-2019-general-election> [Last accessed 28 July 2022].

57   Ibid.

58   Ibid.

59   McInnes, R. (2020) 'General Election 2019: Turnout' <https://commonslibrary. parliament.uk/general-election-2019-turnout/> [Last accessed 28 July 2022].

We Live in a Strange World Where You Can Buy Your Own Truth

60   Alexander Chudik et al., 'Economic Consequences of Covid-19: A Counterfactual Multi-country Analysis', *Vox* (19 October 2020): <https://voxeu.org/article/econo mic-consequences-covid-19-multi-country-analysis> [Last accessed 28 July 2022].

61   *Financial Times*, 'Covid-19: The Global Crisis – in Data' (October 2020): <https://ig.ft.com/coronavirus-global-data/> [Last accessed 28 July 2022].

62   Ayhan Kose and Naotaka Sugawara, 'Understanding the Depth of the 2020 Global Recession in 5 Charts', World Bank Blogs: <https://blogs.worldbank.org/opendata/understanding-depth-2020-global-recession-5-charts> [Last accessed 28 July 2022].

63   *Financial Times*, 'Covid-19: The Global Crisis – in Data'.

64   Office for National Statistics, 'GDP Monthly Estimate, UK: September 2020'; Christian Schulz, 'Global Economic Outlook: Lessons from the Pandemic', *Institute for Fiscal Studies* (October 2020).

65   See, for example, Christian Yates' article in *The Conversation*: Six lessons the UK should have learned, one year on from its first lockdown. Yates quotes formerly a UK Scientific Advisory Group for Emergencies (Sage) member Dr Neil Ferguson as saying that locking down just one week earlier in March 2020 could have saved 20,000 lives – <https://theconversation.com/six-lessons-the-uk-should-have-lear ned-one-year-on-from-its-first-lockdown-157518> [Last accessed 28 July 2022].

66   IMF, Policy Tracker: <https://www.imf.org/en/Topics/imf-and-covid19/Pol icy-Responses-to-COVID-19#C> [Last accessed 28 July 2022].

67   *The Guardian* (December 2020): <https://www.theguardian.com/australia-news/2020/dec/17/australians-trust-in-governments-surges-to-extraordinary-high-amid-covid> [Last accessed 28 July 2022].

68   *Politico* (October 2020): <https://www.politico.eu/article/survey-trust-in-brit ish-government-dropped-to-record-low/> [Last accessed 28 July 2022].

69   Quoted in the British Medical Journal: <https://www.bmj.com/content/370/bmj.m3166> [Last accessed 28 July 2022].

70   'Open Letter to the UK Government Regarding COVID-19': <https://sites.goo gle.com/view/covidopenletter/home> [Last accessed 28 July 2022].

71   Stuart Mills, 'Coronavirus: How the UK Government Is Using Behavioural Science', The Conversation (March 2020): <https://theconversation.com/coronavirus-how-the-uk-government-is-using-behavioural-science-134097> [Last accessed 28 July 2022].

72   This quote is actually taken from Richard Thaler and Cass Sunstein (May 2003), 'Libertarian Paternalism', *The American Economic Review* 93(2), p. 175.

73   Pascale Bourquin and Rowena Crawford (May 2020), 'Automatic Enrolment – Too
      Successful a Nudge to Boost Pension Saving?', Institute for Fiscal Studies: <https://
      www.ifs.org.uk/publications/14850> [Last accessed 28 July 2022].
74   To understand the difference between hard and soft paternalism, we can look at
      obesity. The World Health Organisation, for example, recognises that individual
      choice and responsibility are important in fighting this deadly disease. However,
      'individual responsibility can only have its full effect where people have access to
      a healthy lifestyle'. Therefore, at the societal level it is important to support indi-
      viduals in making dietary and lifestyle changes through 'sustained implementa-
      tion of evidence-based and population-based policies that make regular physical
      activity and healthier dietary choices available, affordable and easily accessible to
      everyone, particularly to the poorest individuals. Does the WHO recommend
      libertarian paternalism or nudging? No. It recommends 'hard' paternalist pol-
      icies like a tax on sugar sweetened beverages. The WHO also challenges the food
      industry to 'play a significant role in promoting healthy diets' by 'reducing the
      fat, sugar and salt content of processed foods; ensuring that healthy and nutri-
      tious choices are available and affordable to all consumers; restricting marketing
      of foods high in sugars, salt and fats, especially those foods aimed at children and
      teenagers; and ensuring the availability of healthy food choices and supporting
      regular physical activity practice in the workplace'. World Health Organization,
      'Obesity and overweight': <https://www.who.int/news-room/fact-sheets/det
      ail/obesity-and-overweight> [Last accessed 28 July 2022].
75   Richard Thaler and Cass Sunstein (2009). *Nudge*, London: Penguin, p. 5.
76   Davies, W. (2017). *The Limits of Neoliberalism: Authority, Sovereignty and the
      Logic of Competition*. London: Sage, p. 162. Conveniently, nudging theory also
      establishes links between the status quo and various biological arguments about
      intelligence, genetics and the normalcy of the patriarchal family – a form of
      'biologism' that Stephen J. Gould traces back to the very earliest forms of capit-
      alist ideology in his classic, *The Mismeasure of Man*.
77   Ibid. p. 163.
78   See, for example, Boas, T. and Gans-Morse, J. (2009). 'Neoliberalism: From New
      Liberal Philosophy to Anti-Liberal Slogan'. *Studies in Comparative International
      Development* 44 (2), pp. 137-61.
79   I use scare quotes here because if we mean by the term 'radical' something like
      'progressive', then neoliberals are the exact opposite, they are reactionary, seeking
      to entrench capitalist social relations even further into everyday life. However, for
      about 40 years, when Keynesianism ruled supreme, neoliberals were considered
      fringe, to say the least. A good example is an argument between Keynes and Hayek
      during the 1930s, during the Great Depression. Keynes insisted that governments
      should spend to stimulate demand, creating jobs that would drive spending in a
      positive feedback loop that would bring economies out of recession. Hayek, by

contrast, insisted that firms and banks should be left to go bust during a crisis, so that the economy be purged of easy money and bad business, returning it to health. With the UK suffering from mass unemployment, Hayek's harsh medicine seemed totally out of touch, and Keynes won the day. There is an interesting reconstruction of this debate on BBC Radio 4, with Keynes' biographer Keynes's biographer, Lord Skidelsky, defending his ideas against modern day Hayekians, which at the time of writing was still available on BBC Sounds: <https://www.bbc.co.uk/sounds/play/b012wxyg> [Last accessed 28 July 2022].

80   Red Vienna refers to a period between 1918 and 1934 when the Austrian capital was controlled by the Social Democratic Workers' Party of Austria (SDAP), which pursued a far-reaching social program including the building of social housing and improving public education, healthcare and sanitation.

81   Hayek, F. A. (1945). 'The Use of Knowledge in Society'. *The American Economic Review* 35 (4), pp. 519–30.

82   Polanyi, M. (1969) *Knowing and Being*. Chicago: University of Chicago Press, p. 156.

83   See in particular Polanyi, M. (1958) *Personal Knowledge*. Chicago: University of Chicago Press.

84   Really the idea of a 'background understanding' is drawn, in my case at least, from the work of Martin Heidegger, via US post-pragmatist Hubert Dreyfus. See Dreyfus, H. L. (1990) *Being-in-the-World: A Commentary on Heidegger's Being in Time, Division I*. Cambridge: MIT Press.

85   See, for example, Kuhn, T. S. (1996) *The Structure of Scientific Revolutions*. Chicago: Chicago University Press

86   Hayek (1945), p. 527.

87   Wainwright, H. (1994). *Arguments for a New Left*. Oxford: Blackwell, p. 5.

88   My 'go to' example is the Lucas Aerospace Combine's Alternative Plan. In the 1970s, a group of highly skilled engineers at various Lucas Aerospace factories came together to challenge the company's corporate plan, which they anticipated would involve mass redundancies. Via a conscious-raising survey and intelligence gathering process, they produced an alternative plan with over 50 products designed to meet social needs. Among the products were revolutionary ecological models commonplace today, such as heat pumps, road-rail vehicles, hydrogen fuel cells. These were ignored because they did not fit the logic of profitable production at the time. The point is that by drawing on the collective intelligence of workers in communities, the combine was able to leap far ahead of its time, and could have put us decades ahead in the race to prevent ecological catastrophe. See Wainwright, H. and Elliott, D. (2018) *The Lucas Plan: A New Trade Unionism in the Making?* Nottingham: Spokesman Books. I have also written about the Lucas Plan, mainly in relation to education: <https://www.redpepper.org.uk/what-can-academics-learn-from-the-lucas-plan/> [Last accessed 28 July 2022]. For an account of Dewey's version of tacit knowledge, see *The Method of Democracy*.

89   As recounted by recent histories of neoliberalism, the Mont Pèlerin Society was
      a clandestine transnational organisation, with links to academia, thinks tanks,
      politicians and the media, whose purpose was the undermining of socialism in
      any form and the promotion of free markets across the world.
90   Quoted in Foucault, M. (2008). *The Birth of Biopolitics: Lectures at the College de
      France, 1978–79*. London: Palgrave MacMillan, p. 121.
91   Ibid, p. 120.
92   See Mirowski, P., and Plehwe, D. (2009). *The Road from Mont Pèlerin: The
      Making of the Neoliberal Thought Collective*. Cambridge: Harvard University
      Press and Burgin, A. (2015) *The Great Persuasion: Reinventing Free Markets Since
      the Depression*. Cambridge: Harvard University Press.
93   Horn, R. V. and Mirowski, P. (2009). 'The Rise of the Chicago School of
      Economics and the Birth of Neoliberalism' in Mirowski, P. and Plehwe, D. (eds),
      The Road from Mont Pèlerin: The Making of the Neoliberal Thought Collective, pp.
      139–78. Cambridge: Harvard University Press.
94   Friedman, M. (2009a) 'The Methodology of Positive Economics' in Mäki U.
      (ed.), *The Methodology of Positive Economics: Milton Friedman's Essay After Half
      a Century*, pp. 3–43. Cambridge: Cambridge University Press.
95   Mäki, U. (2009). 'Reading the Methodological Essay in Twentieth-Century
      Economics: Map of Multiple Perspectives' in Mäki, U. (ed.), *The Methodology
      of Positive Economics: Milton Friedman's Essay After Half a Century*, pp. 47–67.
      Cambridge: Cambridge University Press.
96   Popper, K. (1963). *Conjectures and Refutations*. London: Routledge and Kegan
      Paul.
97   Ibid., p. 36.
98   'Continuity' is another useful Deweyian concept. Dewey was critical of any phil-
      osophy or worldview that mistook the distinctions of analysis with ontological
      or epistemological divisions in reality, or qualitative or revolutionary breaks in
      history.
99   This refers to the 'Trump Wall', the incomplete 700 miles of wall, fence and other
      barriers spanning the 1,954-mile US Mexico border.

But It's the Only World We've Got

100   <https://www.theguardian.com/world/australia-news-blog/video/2014/jan/
      06/dead-bats-queensland-video> [Last accessed 28 July 2022].
101   <https://theconversation.com/killer-climate-tens-of-thousands-of-flying-foxes-
      dead-in-a-day-23227> [Last accessed 28 July 2022].
102   <https://www.bbc.co.uk/news/world-australia-46859000>[Last accessed 28 July
      2022].

103 <https://www.bbc.co.uk/news/world-australia-50951043> [Last accessed 28 July 2022].

104 <https://www.vice.com/en/article/ywkjpw/watch-this-father-and-son-barely-escape-a-wildfire> [Last accessed 28 July 2022].

105 <https://science.sciencemag.org/content/368/6496/1239> [Last accessed 28 July 2022]; <https://www.nationalgeographic.com/environment/article/sea-level-rise-1> [Last accessed 28 July 2022].

106 <https://www.nationalgeographic.com/environment/article/climate-change-drives-migration-crisis-in-bangladesh-from-dhaka-sundabans> [Last accessed 28 July 2022].

107 The best place to find the facts on climate change as they develop is via the IPCC's frequently published reports. This quote is taken from the 'Summary for Policymakers' of the 2018 report, 'Global Warming of 1.5°C. An IPCC Special Report on the impacts of global warming of 1.5°C above pre-industrial levels and related global greenhouse gas emission pathways, in the context of strengthening the global response to the threat of climate change, sustainable development, and efforts to eradicate poverty'. The more recently published AR6 Climate Change 2022: Mitigation of Climate Change outlines the projected impacts of global warming on different parts of the world, and sets out how the measures to both prevent and mitigate their consequence are already available. The reports seem intimidating to read, but are actually very clear.

108 Klein, N. (2014) *This Changes Everything: Capitalism vs. the Climate.* London: Penguin (Epub version).

109 McKie, R. E. (2019) 'Climate Change Counter Movement Neutralization Techniques: A Typology to Examine the Climate Change Counter Movement'. Sociological Inquiry 89, pp. 288-316. <https://doi.org/10.1111/soin.12246>

110 Brulle, R. J. (2014) 'Institutionalizing Delay: Foundation Funding and The creation of U.S. Climate Change Counter-Movement Organizations'. *Climatic Change* 122, pp. 681–94. <https://doi.org/10.1007/s10584-013-1018-7>.

111 <https://corporate.exxonmobil.com/Sustainability/Environmental-protection/Climate-change> [Last accessed 28 July 2022].

112 <https://insideclimatenews.org/news/22122015/exxon-mobil-oil-industry-peers-knew-about-climate-change-dangers-1970s-american-petroleum-institute-api-shell-chevron-texaco/> [Last accessed 28 July 2022].

113 Ibid.

114 <https://www.nationalgeographic.com/environment/article/alberta-canadas-tar-sands-is-growing-but-indigenous-people-fight-back> [Last accessed 28 July 2022]

115 <https://www.ft.com/content/95efca74-4299-11ea-a43a-c4b328d9061c> [Last accessed 28 July 2022].

116 Klein (2014), no page.

117   Foster, J. B. (2017) 'The Long Ecological Revolution'. *Monthly Review* 69(6). Available online: <https://monthlyreview.org/2017/11/01/the-long-ecological-revolution/> [Last accessed 28 July 2022].

118   Gates, B. (2021). *How to Avoid a Climate Disaster: The Solutions We Have and the Breakthroughs We Need.* London: Penguin Books (Epub - no page references available for any of the quotes used below).

119   The Green New Deal Group (2008) 'A Green New Deal: Joined-up Policies to solve the Triple Crunch of the Credit Crisis, Climate Change and High Oil Prices'. Available online: <https://neweconomics.org/2008/07/green-new-deal> [Last accessed 28 July 2022].

120   US Congress (2019) 'RESOLUTION Recognizing the duty of the Federal Government to Create a Green New Deal'. Available online: <https://www.ocasiocortez.com/green-new-deal>.

121   Aronoff, K., Battistoni, A., Cohen, D. A., and Riofrancos, T. (2019) *A Planet to Win: Why We Need a Green New Deal.* London: Verso (Epub – no page references).

122   Marx, K. (1990) *Capital Volume 1.* London: Penguin.

123   Foster (2017).

124   Gramsci, A. (1999). *Selections from the Prison Notebooks of Antonio Gramsci.* London: Lawrence and Wishart.

125   This phrase is taken from Thunberg, G. (2019) *No One is Too Small to Make a Difference.* London: Penguin Books – no page. All Thunberg quotes taken from here, as are the titles of the chapters of the book.

126   <https://fridaysforfuture.org/take-action/how-to-strike/> [Last accessed 28 July 2022] - Thunberg also calls for adults to 'take your place in the streets striking for your work'. This indicates that the Youth Climate Strike is a political use of the strike weapon, one that points more to a general strike capable of effecting systemic political and economic change, rather than the limited economic strikes aimed at wage increases or workplace improvements.

127   <https://www.climaterealityproject.org/blog/zero-hour-meet-16-year-old-leading-next-climate-march> [Last accessed 28 July 2022].

128   <https://www.theguardian.com/commentisfree/2018/oct/06/i-sued-the-state-of-washington-because-i-cant-breathe-there-they-ignored-me> [Last accessed 28 July 2022].

129   <https://www.seattletimes.com/seattle-news/environment/seattles-jamie-margolin-is-17-and-a-climate-activist-on-wednesday-she-testifies-before-congress/> [Last accessed 28 July 2022].

130   <https://www.theguardian.com/us-news/2017/jan/24/keystone-xl-dakota-access-pipelines-revived-trump-administration> [Last accessed 28 July 2022].

131   He has, in fact, said he *won't* stop construction: <https://earthjustice.org/brief/2021/biden-delivers-disappointment-on-the-dakota-access-pipeline> [Last accessed 28 July 2022].

We Are Fighting for Everyone's Future

132 Foucault (2008).
133 Rashdall, H. (1895) *The Universities of Europe on the Middle Ages*. Oxford: Clarendon Press, pp. 335-8.
134 Cobban, A. B. (1971) 'Medieval Student Power'. *Past & Present* 53, pp. 28-66.
135 Anderson, R. D. (2004) *European Universities from the Enlightenment to 1914*. Oxford: Oxford University Press.
136 Kant, I. (2017) 'The Conflict of the Philosophy Faculty with the Theology Faculty' in Peters, M. A. and Barnett, R. (eds), *The Idea of the University*. Bern: Peter Lang, p. 5.
137 Anderson (2004), p. 52.
138 Kant, I. (1784) 'What is Enlightenment'. Available from: <http://www.colum bia.edu/acis/ets/CCREAD/etscc/kant.html> [Last accessed 28 July 2022].
139 Kant (1784). In this essay, meant for public consumption, Kant curbs the worst of his intellectual elitism. But in his essay on the university (Kant, 2017) he expresses a low opinion not just of scholars in other faculties, but of the people as a 'civil community'. 'The people want to be led,' Kant insists, 'they want to be *duped* (my emphasis).' This kind of manipulation is fine for the lazy and cowardly masses, but not for the public, which Kant associates with a 'learned community devoted to the sciences', or what he calls in the Enlightenment essay, the 'reading public'.
140 This sentence refers to two, complementary critiques of bourgeois culture: Jürgen Habermas' *The Structural Transformation of the Public Sphere* (1989, Polity Press) and Bourdieu and Passeron's 'Cultural and Social Reproduction', which can be found in Richard Brown's edited collection, *Knowledge, Education, and Cultural Change: Papers in the Sociology of Education* (2018, Routledge). See also Chapter 1
141 Bourdieu, P. (1986) 'Forms of Capital', in Richardson, J., *Handbook of Theory and Research for the Sociology of Education*, Westport: Greenwood, pp. 241–58.
142 Committee on Higher Education (1963) 'Report of the Committee appointed by the Prime Minister under the Chairmanship of Lord Robbins'. Available from: <http://www.educationengland.org.uk/documents/robbins/robbins1963.html> [Last accessed 28 July 2022].
143 Holmwood, J. (2014). 'From Social Rights to the Market: Neoliberalism and the Knowledge Economy', *International Journal of Lifelong Education* 33 (1), p. 66.
144 Marshall, T. H. (1992) *Citizenship and Social Class*. London: Pluto Press, p. 8.
145 Russell, C. (2013) 'Human Capital Theory', in Ainsworth J. (ed.), *Sociology of Education: An A-To-Z Guide Vol. 1*. London: SAGE Publications, pp. 369-9.
146 Ibid.
147 Committee on Higher Education (1963), p. 205.

148 Willetts, D. (2017) *A University Education*. Oxford: Oxford University Press, p. 74.
149 McGettigan, A. (2015) 'The Treasury View of Higher Education', PERC Paper 6. Available from <https://www.perc.org.uk/project_posts/perc-paper-the-treas ury-view-of-higher-education-by-andrew-mcgettigan/>[Lastaccessed28July2022].
150 See, for example, the Trades Union Congress report, 'A just transition to a greener, fairer economy'. Like the Green New Deal, the concept of 'just transition' has been hijacked by progressive neoliberals to mean just about anything to do with green capitalism. But in its original formulation, this is all about making sure that no one is left behind in the move to 'net zero' – crucial in winning over trade unions and workers in 'dirty' industries like coal, oil and gas.
151 I point you back to the Lucas Plan, see fn 88.
152 See, for example: Ridley, D. (2019) 'Can Universities Become 'Anchors' for a Green Economy?': <http://classonline.org.uk/blog/item/can-universities-bec ome-anchors-for-a-green-economy> [Last accessed 28 July 2022].
     Ridley, D. (2020) 'Four (Big) Steps to Save Our Universities': <https://weownit. org.uk/blog/four-big-steps-save-our-universities> [Last accessed 28 July 2022]; Ridley, D. (2021) 'We Are Fighting for Everyone's Future', Post-16 Educator 105, pp. 14-18: <http://post16educator.org.uk/psearchive/> [Last accessed 28 July 2022].

Index

Printed in Great Britain
by Amazon

11756366R00058